Month by Month, Day by Day, Make Your Dreams Come True!

Let Dr. Robert Schuller guide you through a year of change to a triumphant new life:

January—A new you in the New Year.
February—There is a miracle to match your dream.
March—It's Lent. Let's eliminate negative
        thinking.
April—Someday is today.
May—Chains or change.
June—Make your dreams materialize.
July—Strive to come alive.
August—Problems are masked possibilities.
September—Put God's power to work today.
October—God's gifts to you.
November—Tap into trust (and take the truth test).
December—The miracle of love's rewards.

Living Powerfully One Day at a Time

"Treat yourself from January 1 to December 31 with one of Dr. Schuller's messages every day and life will be different, for you will be different."
                                        —*Norman Vincent Peale*

Also by Robert H. Schuller from Jove

MOVE AHEAD WITH POSSIBILITY THINKING
PEACE OF MIND THROUGH POSSIBILITY THINKING
THE PEAK TO PEEK PRINCIPLE
POWER IDEAS FOR A HAPPY FAMILY
YOU CAN BECOME THE PERSON YOU WANT TO BE
DAILY POWER THOUGHTS
SELF-LOVE
SELF-ESTEEM
LIVING POSITIVELY ONE DAY AT A TIME

Most Jove Books are available at special quantity discounts for bulk pur-
chases for sales promotions, premiums, fund raising, or educational use.
Special books or book excerpts can also be created to fit specific needs.

For details, write or telephone Special Sales Markets, The Berkley Publishing
Group, 200 Madison Avenue, New York, New York 10016; (212) 686-9820.

ROBERT H. SCHULLER

LIVING POWERFULLY ONE DAY AT A TIME

POWER THOUGHTS FOR EACH DAY OF THE YEAR

A JOVE BOOK

This Jove book contains the complete
text of the original edition.

LIVING POWERFULLY ONE DAY AT A TIME

A Jove Book / published by arrangement with
Fleming H. Revell Company

PRINTING HISTORY
Crystal Cathedral Ministries edition published 1982
Fleming H. Revell edition / February 1983
Jove edition / January 1986
Second printing / March 1986
Third printing / May 1986

ISBN: 0-515-08443-3

Jove Books are published by The Berkley Publishing Group,
200 Madison Avenue, New York, N.Y. 10016.
The words "A JOVE BOOK" and the "J" with sunburst
are trademarks belonging to Jove Publications, Inc.

PRINTED IN THE UNITED STATES OF AMERICA

Introduction

It never fails that as I travel around the country and meet people who have been touched by the Hour of Power ministry so many of them credit the positive lives they lead to a daily focus on the great truth found in the Bible. To live positively means to feel good about yourself, and how do you feel good about yourself? You get to know someone who truly loves you. My friend, I suggest that the one who knows and loves you more than anyone else is the living loving person of Jesus Christ. My hope is that as you read these daily guides, you will get to know Him better. And as you do you will discover how to live positively—one day at a time.

CONTENTS

JANUARY—   A NEW YOU IN THE NEW YEAR
       A New Year for a New You
       A New Day for a New You
       A New Day for a New Way
       A New Day for a New Dream
       A New Day for a New Heart
       A New Day for a Fresh Start

FEBRUARY—   THERE IS A MIRACLE TO MATCH
       YOUR DREAM
       A Miracle Every Day
       Meet the Miracle Maker
       The Miracle of Self-Discovery
       A Miracle of Love

MARCH—   IT'S LENT—LET'S ELIMINATE
       NEGATIVE THINKING
       Let's Add Faith
       Let's Add Risk
       Let's Add Prayer
       Let's Add Style

APRIL—   SOMEDAY IS TODAY
       Someday Is Salvation
       Someday Is Inspired
       Trust God for Someday
       Believe in Someday
       Someday Is Possible—Someday Is Today!

MAY—   CHAINS OR CHANGE
       Change Your Heart
       Change Your Moods
       Change Your Thoughts
       Change Your Destiny

JUNE—   MAKE YOUR DREAMS MATERIALIZE
       Possibilitize
       Sterilize
       Tranquilize
       Harmonize
       Actualize

JULY—   STRIVE TO COME ALIVE
                Strive to Abide
                I'll Survive
                I'll Thrive
                I'll Arrive
                I'll Come Alive
AUGUST—   PROBLEMS ARE MASKED
                POSSIBILITIES
                Fruitful Frustrations
                Welcome Interruptions
                Creative Competition
                The Greatest Possibility Thinker
SEPTEMBER—   PUT GOD'S POWER TO WORK TODAY
                Relieving Power
                Believing Power
                Transforming Power
                Character-Building Power
                Achieving Power
OCTOBER—   GOD'S GIFTS TO YOU
                Faith
                Confidence and Enthusiasm
                Courage and Perseverance
                Patience and Forgiveness
                Peace
NOVEMBER—   TAP INTO TRUST
                Take the Trust Test
                The Thrust of the Trust
                Trust means "Let Go and Let God"
                Nest, Test, Invest, Arrest, and Crest
DECEMBER—   THE MIRACLE OF LOVE'S REWARDS
                Love Conquers Fear
                Love Expects the Best
                Love: the Source of Joy
                Love: the Greatest Gift

LIVING POWERFULLY ONE DAY AT A TIME

A New You in the New Year

A New Year for a New You

"I am come that they might have life, and that they might have it more abundantly."

John 10:10

Every new year is like the beginning of a totally new life! That's exciting! Today is really the first day of the rest of your life. It's a chance to begin all over again.

Awhile back I was interviewed in a radio station in Chicago, Illinois. There was just the interviewer and myself in a little radio room. We looked through a glass window at the engineer, who threw us the signal to begin. The interviewer began . . . "We have with us today, Dr. Robert Schuller, etc., etc., etc. . . ." Then he asked me a question. Just after he had asked the question, he clapped his hands and said, "I'm sorry, the engineer is telling me that something didn't go right. We'll have to start over." He looked at the engineer and said, "Let's go again in about five minutes." Then he turned to me and remarked, "This is a chance to start over. You know," he added, "it isn't often in life that you get a chance to start clean over again."

After five minutes the engineer gave the signal and we started again. "Good morning, we have with us today, Dr. Robert Schuller, etc., etc., etc. . . ."

It isn't often in life that you get a chance to start all over again. I believe that every day is a chance to start all over again. Start living a new life today! A New You in the New Year!

**Today is the first day of the rest of my life.
I choose to live abundantly!**

A New Year for a New You

"As Christ was raised from the dead by the glory of the Father, we, too, might walk in newness of life."

Romans 6:4

As my wife and I were sailing down an Italian road, in a hurry to see the sights, we realized we had to cash a traveler's check into Italian money. Suddenly, the traffic started slowing down, and across the eight-lane highway, we saw toll gates. Now of course we didn't expect a toll road, and it was too late to turn around. So I asked my wife, "Do you think they'll take American dollars?" She only laughed. "How about traveler's checks?" I asked. She laughed again.

Well, as it turned out, they only took Italian money. But before we knew it, God had a solution to the problem. As we waited for the cars ahead to go through the toll gate, we stopped our car. As the car ahead of us drove on, we tried to move ahead only to find that our car wouldn't move. No matter what we tried, it wouldn't budge. As we sat there, people drove around us, shouting angry words. Finally, after an hour, a tow truck came to our rescue, and took us to a repair shop. The smoke was pouring from the back wheels by this time, as all four brakes were frozen.

There are many people who are stuck like that right now on the freeway of life. Maybe you've got the feeling that you are not moving ahead . . . you're frozen where you are . . . traffic is passing you by.

Let Jesus come in and unlock the wheels. You, too, can start rolling again!

> **Today I will let Jesus thaw the frozen possibilities that I have allowed to lay dormant in my life. I will begin to move to a new me!**

A New Day for a New You

"What can we ever say to such wonderful things as these? If God is on our side, who can ever be against us?"

Romans 8:31

Did you know that your whole future is not in God's hands but in yours! You hold the key! What's going to happen will depend upon one person—the person who sets your sights. Who sets your sights? Who sets your goals? The key to your future is within you. You hold it, whether you know it or not.

God has a beautiful future for you! *The key is inside of you!* You can open the door—it's unlocked. Simply allow yourself to see the person God wants you to be.

The person who lifts you up—more than anybody else—is the person who lifts your sights, sets your goals, and makes your plans. In the same way, nobody puts you down more than the person who lowers your sights, lowers your goals, and makes little plans for your future. Who is this person? This person is you!

Today, here and now, make this resolution: *Never again will I put myself down.* God made me; Jesus Christ died for me. God believes in me. I'm going to start believing in what God believes in. I'm going to believe in me!

> **My future is in my hands.**
> **I will trust God to help me make the most of it!**

A New Day for a New You

"The kingdom of God is within you."

Luke 17:21

Do you know what every mother asks when her new baby is born? The first question is always, "Is my baby all right?" They want to know if the baby has all the fingers and toes. But the biggest question is one they don't have to ask: "Doctor, does my baby have wings in his heart?" The truth is, all God's children are born with wings in their hearts and in their souls. The tragedy is that some people go through life and never discover the possibility of inner lifting power. So they never really fly; they remain earthbound. Of all tragedies, this is the greatest. We are experiencing problems today because of waste. We waste energy, we waste gas, and we waste money. But the greatest waste of all is the waste of life's undiscovered potential.

God built wings in you—discover them, open them, and fly. Our Lord Jesus Christ said, *"The kingdom of God is within you."* Within you! You can be a beautiful person. Yes, you! . . . in spite of your sins, your shortcomings, your frailties, your faults. Deep down, within your heart, there are wings waiting to be unfolded and stretched. Give yourself soul power. Indeed it is there, waiting to come out.

Jesus offers you something beyond success. He offers you happiness! Success, you know, is getting what you want. Happiness is wanting what you get.

> **Today I will fly through my day on soul power— on God's power!**

A New Day for a New You

"Blessed are the eyes which see what you see!"

Luke 10:23

One morning I stopped for breakfast in a little restaurant. A man came up to me and asked, "Excuse me, sir, is your name Dr. Schuller?" I answered, "Yes." He was a tall, good-looking man. He introduced himself as Wayne Reploge, from the University of Kansas. "You know, Dr. Schuller, every summer for 45 years, I have been a guide at Yellowstone Park. Some years ago I reached the top, which means that the celebrities and internationally famous people who come to see the park are assigned to me."

"It must be a thrilling job to take all these people through the park and listen to their exclamations of joy," I commented. "That's what I want to tell you," he continued. "You would not believe how many people I have taken through Yellowstone Park who barely say, 'Thank you.' They come through with a ho-hum attitude. They were looking at their watches. They couldn't wait to go. They said nothing positive about the whole thing at all. It used to get me down. Now, for the last several years, before I take them through I say, 'Before we go out there, I want to tell you something. *There is nothing out there at all to see. There is nothing there. It is all inside of you.* And if it isn't inside you, you will see nothing there. But if it is truly there, you'll be excited when you see the mountain peaks. And when the geysers erupt. It's all inside of you!' "

> My life will be beautiful or it will be ugly.
> It all depends on how I choose to look on it.
> Choose beauty today!

A New Day for a New You

"As therefore you received Christ Jesus the Lord, so live in him, rooted and built up in him and established in the faith."
Colossians 2:6,7

The kingdom of God is within you. You have probably heard of or seen the golden Buddha in Bangkok. For 1,000 years the biggest solid chunk of sculptured gold in the world was lost, hidden behind a rough concrete shell that the creators of the golden Buddha had built around it to protect it and hide it from invading armies. For 1,000 years this huge, solid gold Buddha was hidden in cement. In 1957 it was accidently dropped from a crane, cracked, and the inner splendor was discovered.

There is within you a treasure waiting to be discovered. How do you realize that treasure within you? How can you release God's power?

Crack the crust that keeps God's power locked up. All your rejections, your failures, your hurts, your defeats tend to accumulate like encrustations around your inner spirit, until some people, as they begin to get old, turn more negative and more unbelieving.

Crack the crust on your fears, your hurts, and your rejections, and let God get in.

> Today, O Lord, chip away my fears and fill me
> with belief, strip away my hurts
> and soothe me deep within.

A New Day for a New You

"I can do all things through Christ who strengthens me."
Philippians 4:13

We have in our home one of those big, heavy, fireproof safes. We don't have any good jewelry to put in it, but what we have in it are important papers, like birth certificates, passports, that sort of thing. One day I needed one of those papers. I asked my wife, "Will you get it for me, it's in the safe." She replied, "I don't know where the key is." We could not find the key, even after a thorough search. So I finally put the safe in the trunk of my car and drove to a locksmith.

He looked at it and said, "I think I can find a key for that." He returned with some keys, but none of them fit the lock. He tried a few more keys, but with no luck. He said, "I really don't know much about this business, I am only temporary here today. The owner will be in tomorrow . . . if you could bring it back . . ." And as he lifted it, he grabbed the edge underneath the lid and the lid opened up! It was unlocked all the time! And right on top, inside, was the key!

The key to a new you is inside you, right now! You can choose to take it and unlock your God-given possibilities!

The key to a new me is in my hands—
RIGHT NOW!

A New Day for a New You

"Seek ye first the kingdom of God, and his righteousness, and all these things shall be added unto you."

Matthew 6:33

This year begin each new day by asking yourself, "Lord, am I the person you want me to be? How can I become the person you want me to be? God, where should I make changes today in my life? Show me where I've got a hang-up. Show me where I've been stubborn. Show me where I would not listen." There isn't a person alive who doesn't have a hang-up. I know none of us are living perfect lives.

So pray, "God, I'm willing to make changes, I'm willing to make sacrifices, I'm willing to make commitments, I'm willing to make decisions if it's what you want. I'm willing to listen to You." People who never change their minds are either perfect to begin with or stubborn forever after. I know I'm not perfect, and I sure don't want to be stubborn. So I will ask the Lord to change my mind.

Today, Lord, my prayer is this:

> As I start to pray right,
> I will begin to live right.

19

A New Day for a New You

"Unless a grain of wheat falls into the earth and dies, it remains alone; but if it dies it bears much fruit."

John 12:24

If you pray the right prayer, be prepared to *pay the right price.* God will always attach a price to a dream. He promises that a kernel of seed can be fruitful and multiply itself a thousandfold. That's His promise. Then the seed has to pay the price and the price is death. It has to go in the ground.

I cannot tell you that if you simply pray the right prayer, God will make all your dreams come true. But pray the right prayer and God will give you the key. Then you have to pay the price. Many people are not enjoying health today because they don't want to pay the price. They do not eat right. They do not drink right. They eat foods that hurt their health. They drink too much coffee, tea, or alcoholic beverages. They pollute their lungs with tobacco. They do not discipline themselves.

I can tell you the basic keys to health and happiness are in your soul and in your heart. But, are you willing to pay the price? Have you given your life to Jesus Christ? You admire Him, you respect Him, you salute Him. You think He's marvelous, and you are very happy when you hear other people say how they have given their lives to the Lord. Today's a new day—a new chance to try a new way—God's way!

> **Success is not cheap. Today I will pay the price of my time to help someone who is hurting.**

A New Day for a New Way

"My God shall supply your every need."

Philippians 4:19

First pray the right prayer and then pay the right price. Now—get set to: *Play the right game.* This means that you become a participant and not a spectator. It means you get out of the grandstands and get your uniform on and get on the field. It means you stop applauding and start making commitments. If you are going to get into a relationship with the Lord, you have to take action and make a commitment.

When you get ready to play the game of prosperity with God, the first thing He says to you is, "It's your move. You start."

Is your soul right with Jesus Christ? It's an all important question. I invite you now to pray the right prayer and pay the right price and be willing to surrender yourself—make a commitment to Jesus Christ—make the first move to a new you.

Make the decision based not upon your ability but upon God's ability. Make your move. And then God will make His, and miracles will begin to happen. Do it now!

> Lord, direct the changes so that I shall be
> more and more like You.

A New Day for a New Way

"Do not be conformed to this world but be transformed by the renewal of your mind that you may prove what is the will of God, what is good and acceptable and perfect."

Romans 12:2

I have a favorite radio station that I listen to. When I am traveling, one of the things I miss most is that I can't pick up my favorite station. Is the station dead? Is it not functioning? Or is my radio no good? The radio is good, the station is on the air, I'm just too far away to pick up the signal, that's all.

Can you hear God's voice? Are you in tune with God's Spirit? If you want to feel God's power in your life, if you want to unlock your possibilities, and if you want to find a new you, then you have to get in tune with God's Spirit, and in line with God's will, obey Him. How? By listening to positive thoughts not to negative thoughts. It's that simple. God will speak to you through positive thoughts, not negative thoughts.

Do you know that God has powers within you, waiting to be tapped through Christ's Holy Spirit? Powers that can work miracles you've never experienced before.

You have power built in you. Get in touch with God's Spirit. Get in line with His will. Let God's power flow through you. Try possibility thinking! It will release powers you never knew you had.

> **Tune in to God and
> tune in on life.**

A New Day for a New Way

"By this we know love, that he laid down his life for us; and we ought to lay down our lives for the brethren."

1 John 3:16

Tune in to God's Spirit. And then get in touch with God's people. Because you're in tune with His Spirit, He'll give you a big idea, a wonderful dream, and believe me, that dream will be too big for you to handle alone. If you get a dream and it's so small you can tackle it all by yourself, it has not come from God. When God gives you His dream, it'll be more than you can do by yourself. And God sets it up that way to keep us humble so that when the big things happen, we can never say, "I did it all by myself." It forces you to ask for help, and that's very humbling.

1. Is my dream big enough to require help?

2. If so—where do I need help the most?

3. Who can help me?

4. Who can I help?

> **Thank You, Lord, for all the people**
> **You have in mind who will help me today,**
> **and whom I will help!**

A New Day for a New Way

"Let me hear in the morning of thy steadfast love, for in thee I put my trust. Teach me the way I should go, for to thee I lift up my soul."

Psalms 143:8

Get in tune with God's Spirit, He'll give you a dream. Get in touch with God's people; ask them for help. It'll be humbling, and that's good. God's people will make it happen. Then—get in time with God's calendar. Once I preached a message on prayer, and I shared four answers God can give: When the request is not right, God says, "No." When you are not right, God says, "Grow." When the time is not right, God says, "Slow." When everything is right, God says, "Go."

Sometimes it means we have to move a lot faster than we had planned. Sometimes it means we have to wait and wait until God is ready.

God has a plan for every life. God has a plan for you. You need a dream. A person who has a dream is truly alive—enthusiastic, exciting, and energetic—because there is a purpose for living.

If you want your dream to become a reality you must (1) be sure it's the right dream, then (2) be sure that you are right for the dream, and (3) be aware of God's timing—you may have to suddenly run, or you may have to wait patiently, but when God says, "Go," He says, "Go"—and before you know it your dreams will glow with reality.

Am I ready to run when God says, "Go?"
Make me willing to go where He sends me.

A New Day for a New Way

"Let us strip off anything that slows us down or holds us back; and let us run with patience the particular race that God has set before us."

Hebrews 12:1

Today is a new day for a new you. Today is a valuable day and not one minute of it can be wasted. God has plans for you today to help you make your dreams come true.

What can you do today to make you a new you?

What can you do today to help your dream come true?

What are You up to today, O Lord? I want to be part of it.

Show me, dear God, what You are up to today— make me a part of it—make me aware of Your leading.

A New Day for a New Way

"Where there is no vision, the people perish."

Proverbs 29:18

My secretaries have a little note over their typewriters that reads: *Nobody has any business feeling helpless, hopeless, and unneeded in a world where there is so much hurt.*

There are so many people who are so confused, so broken, and so empty that they have to depend upon a box, a bottle, pills, or illicit sex. No person has the right to feel helpless, hopeless, and unneeded when so many people are lonely! So you can find a dream to be helpful, too! Everybody needs a dream.

"Where there is no vision, the people perish." Modern psychiatry says the same thing. Viktor Frankl, the Austrian psychiatrist, spent some time with me a few years ago. He said, "People who do not have goals and dreams are virtually spiritually dead." Will Rogers really said the same thing to young people when he said, "What you need most of all is hard work and an exciting dream." Why is it that people don't have dreams? I submit that it is because they don't dare to dream because they're afraid they'll fail. I want to share with you how you can be assured that you'll succeed with God's dream. I want to share with you how you can have power to make your dreams come true!

Dare to dream—you can do it!
You can help somebody!

A New Day for a New Way

"Surely goodness and mercy shall follow me all the days of my life."

Psalms 23:6

Let me ask you this question: What dreams would you have for your life today, and what plans would you have on your drawing board, and what goals would you be committing yourself to if *you knew you could not fail?* And what dreams would you have if you knew that if you failed you'd receive a crown and a trophy, because in your failure you dared to try to do something beautiful for God? When you find God's dream for your life, it is impossible to fail unless you decide you want to fail.

Dr. Steinberg, the eminent child psychiatrist, has told us, "Most people who fail, fail because they really want to fail. They are trying to pay a price for guilt in some cases, or they are probably trying to punish their parents or they have a childhood fear of competition. Competition to them is a threat, and that frightens them, so they back away and accept failure. But life is structured in such a way that just because we may back away does not mean we won't find ourselves in competitively threatening experiences."

Dare to try—and don't back away—try to do something beautiful for God.

> **God wants me
> to succeed!**

A New Day for a New Dream

"But thanks be to God who, in Christ, always leads us in triumph, and through us spreads the fragrance of the knowledge of him everywhere."

2 Corinthians 2:14

God has a dream and He wants you to grab hold of it. And your dream can come true if it passes five simple principles. The first principle is below, the next four I'll give you in the next four days.

1. *Try it.* By that I mean, test it. Ask the question, is this God's dream for my life? Is this what He wants me to do?

I have these basic questions to test our dreams by. Is it really needed? In other words, does this bright dream fill a vital human need? Does it help people who are hurting? The secret of success is to find a need and fill it. Now what does that mean? That goals are not ego trips. They are the fulfillment of a deep urge to help people who need to be helped.

The source of dreams and goals must be an unmet human need. Try it and test your dream. Can I really help people who are hurting? Could it inspire? Could it be beautiful? Unless it's beautiful it violates something deep in the human spirit. Will it excel? Can I do it a little better and more beautifully than it's ever been done before? A positive idea that's God's idea deserves to be treated, without spot or wrinkle, perfectly. 1. Try it!

Try it—today!

A New Day for a New Dream

"Your young men shall see visions and your old men shall dream dreams."

Acts 2:17

Once you have *tried it,* then you have to *Eye it.* Visualize your dream, write it down, draw a picture, put it on a board, stick it on your mirror, but get a picture. Eye it, visualize it. It is when you begin to see it in your mind that it becomes a fact.

The other day I was reading Dr. Norman Vincent Peale's book *Positive Principles Today.* In it he says, "If you can visualize it and hold it for two years, it will come to pass." And I believe this. Two years ago, the Crystal Cathedral seemed like an impossibility. Today it stands—a beautiful monument to the power of God and the power of positive visualizing. I saw the Cathedral clearly in my mind—for years before it was built. You may have believed in that dream as well.

What are your dreams for this new year? Eye them, believe in them—they can come true! Each can become a real possibility if you will try it and then eye it!

Take one detail of your dream and describe it right here and now! 2. Eye it!

I'm beginning to see my dream coming true!

A New Day for a New Dream

"Commit your way to the Lord; trust in him, and he will act."
Psalms 37:5

Yesterday we visualized our dream, we described it, and wrote it out in detail—we *eyed it!* Today, we must 3. *Buy it!* Which simply means to make the commitment. If this is God's dream and it is God's idea for your life and you've tried it and eyed it, the third thing is to buy it. That means you make the commitment *before* you have solved all the problems. Be totally sold on the idea. Be willing to pay the price. Every time I have moved ahead to something great for God—a new sanctuary, the Tower of Hope, the Crystal Cathedral, the Hour of Power Television Ministry—at every point I was so convinced that it was God's idea that I would have gladly died for the success of the dream. And when you are so sold on a dream that you would gladly die for it, world—get out of the way! Nothing can stop one who (1) knows, "this is God's dream." And (2) knows "if I drop the ball, I will commit sacrilege to my Lord by spoiling one of the ideas He gave like a jewel."

Try it, eye it and 3. Buy it!

**I commit myself to God's dream for life.
That means—I will not quit!**

A New Day for a New Dream

"Let us run with perseverance the race that is set before us."
Hebrews 12:1

There are many children who every year go down to the nearest store and pick out a special kite. They carefully make a tail for it out of old rags and attach it to a big bundle of string. Now, the child has his dream of flying a kite, but unless he gets out and starts to run, the wind will never catch that kite to carry it high, high, higher into the air.

So it is when you catch a dream. You try it, you eye it, you buy it, and then you 4. *Fly it.* That simply means to begin. Like a little boy with a kite, start running and see if it can catch the wind, and before you know it, the positive idea is yours. People whom you never would have dreamed of will come to your support. The Crystal Cathedral was built by people across the United States that I never would have thought would be so generous. It's true! *Positive ideas attract support from the most unexpected places.*

Today—I will begin to fly my dream. The first steps I can take are:

_____

_____

_____

_____

4. Fly it!

> **If I will take the first step, God will move me**
> **higher and help my dreams to fly!**

A New Day for a New Dream

"Keep traveling steadily along his pathway and in due season he will honor you with every blessing."

Psalms 37:34

Don't quit. Dreams have an enormous inclination to want to drift away when frustration and despair move in and discouragement comes. Try it; test your dream out. Eye it, visualize it. Buy it. Fly it and finally—5. *Tie it down.* Follow all these principles and you will find the power to make your dreams come true.

Stanley Reimer is a very dear friend of mine. A few years ago he suffered a severe heart attack, a *twenty-minute* cardiac arrest. When he arrived at the hospital he was in a comatose condition. The doctors were sure that there was no hope for him. They offered no possibility of even life, to say nothing of recovery. I went to his bedside as soon as I could. I remembered the eminent psychiatrist Dr. Smiley Blanton and what he told me, "Bob, I've been a psychiatrist all my life and I've learned one thing: there are vast undamaged areas in the most severely damaged brain." So I assumed that the same was true for Stan. I told him, "Stan, this is Dr. Schuller. You're going to get well." And a tear rolled out of his eye, the first sign of hope. In his comatose condition, he got a dream that he would recover.

In a few months, Stan came home for a weekend, and I saw him walking *without crutches!* I hugged him and all he could say was, "I love you, I love you."

God is great! He won't let your dream come tumbling down!

I will tie my dreams to God's power when frustrations threaten to blow them away.

A New Day for a New Dream

"God deals with you as with sons; for what son is there whom his father does not discipline?"

Hebrews 12:7

Have you dreamed before—and given it everything you had, just to see your dream die and come crashing down? Are you afraid to dream again for fear you'll fail again? Remember—only you can kill a dream. God never sends anybody to hell. People only decide to send themselves there by turning their backs on salvation.

Perhaps your other dream was not right. Or maybe the time was not right. Or perhaps you were not right.

1. Is it possible your dream was not God's dream?

2. Was there some area in *your life that needed changing in order to see your dream come true?*

3. You are not the same now, nor are you in the same circumstances, life is always changing, and so are you.

4. Do you see where maybe you could be a success today as a more mature, experienced person than you could yesterday?

God has a dream for your life! Don't let past disappointments hold you back from future fulfillments. This is a new year, a new day, and you are a new you.

God doesn't say, "No."
He does say, "Grow!"

A New Day for a New Dream

"For it is God who is at work within you, giving you the will and the power to achieve His purpose."

Philippians 2:13

A new you in the new year. The new you will not fail. Today you are more experienced, more humble. You have learned from your mistakes and will be more willing to accept help. You have learned to rely on God's Spirit and to keep in touch with His guidance.

I remember when I was on the western border of China, way up in the Himalaya Mountains, and I picked up an English voice speaking on a little radio that I was trying to tune. The static was so bad I couldn't quite hear it, which was very frustrating. I could hear a message in English but only a few words. I tuned it and tuned it, but never got it.

God is the dreamer of great dreams, and to get His dream for your life you have to tune in to His Spirit. The new you will not fail, because you have learned the value of tuning your life into God's wavelength. Your dreams are His dreams—and His dreams always succeed!

The new you says, "God, do what You want to with my one life." Now believe me, that prayer will revolutionize you, your dreams, and your life. You will find blessings and success that would otherwise have eluded you.

> I will let God live and dwell in my thoughts,
> in my dreams, and in my pursuits today.

A New Day for a New Heart

"Your body is a temple of the Holy Spirit."

1 Corinthians 6:19

The Bible is filled with many statements indicating that our relationship to God vitally affects our human energy output. Obviously, there is a difference in energy levels from one person to another. The question is "Why?" Now, of course, there is such a thing as having a healthy body. If you don't eat right, or exercise right, you can expect your energy output to suffer drastically.

Since I've been on a physical fitness program and have been running six or seven miles a morning, I feel great. The way to get energy is through physical exercise. After you've run about two miles, strength comes, and then after three miles you have even more energy. When you've finished four miles, you're really ready to go. So many people lack the energy level because they have not been willing to pay the price in disciplining their bodies. "Your body is a temple of the Holy Spirit." If you keep your body in good shape, then the Holy Spirit can live there. The Holy Spirit is the source of our tremendous emotional energy.

If you, too, want to succeed, make sure your energy tank is full. Fill it every day with God's Spirit, and keep yourself finely tuned—both physically and spiritually.

Fill up on God's fuel today—and run like you've never run before!

A New Day for a New Heart

"They who wait upon the Lord shall renew their strength, they shall mount up with wings like eagles, they shall run and not be weary, they shall walk and not faint."

Isaiah 40:31

Energy level is an attitude. I see some people who have a low energy level and they say, "Well, I guess I'm getting old." I can tell you, I've done a lot of research on this for several years. I've been on university campuses where I've seen average students probably twenty to twenty-one years of age, walking slowly, talking slowly, their bodies drooping. If you tinted their hair white and put some lines on their faces, you'd say they were eighty years old. They walk old and talk old.

And I have, by contrast, seen people who are in their seventies and eighties and nineties who walk fast, think fast, talk fast, and live fast. It's more a matter of attitude than it is of age. That's why I don't look at the calendar when I talk about aging. Don't look at the calendar, look at your own heart. All you need to have is one secret, gnawing guilt or sin, and the fear of its exposure can create an emotional block that can reduce your energy output.

Final check: Any secret that you've harbored—a secret that you need to feel God's forgiveness for?

> **Positive thoughts produce emotional and physical power!**

A New Day for a New Heart

"That out of his glorious, unlimited resources he will give you the mighty inner strengthening of his Holy Spirit."
Ephesians 3:16

I was on a television show recently and the interviewer asked, "Dr. Schuller, why do you always seem to be so energetic?" I said, "I suppose I'm energetic because I'm enthusiastic. I suppose I'm enthusiastic because I'm basically a very joyful, happy person." The interviewer pressed, "Yes, but is it reasonable to expect that most people can be happy the way you say you're happy?" I answered, "I think so. I really do. I think if you live right, think right, pray right, love right, give right, and act right, you can't help but be bubbling over with energy. Most people who aren't enthusiastic probably aren't living right. They are guilty, or they're not loving right, or they're angry inside with people. *If you fight battles in your thoughts all day, you can expect to suffer battle fatigue at night.*

I couldn't possibly harbor a secret sin. It would fatigue me. And a great deal of human fatigue is nothing more than a subconscious defense mechanism of a threatened emotional system that doesn't want to run the risk of exposure. *Only the authentic, honest person can be enthusiastic.* Think of that! Why aren't more people genuinely enthusiastic? Because they're not honest.

> **Enthusiasm comes from God—bubbling up and out of me. Experience enthusiasm today!**

A New Day for a New Heart

"He who has the Son has life."

1 John 5:12

Love is an energy-producing force. When you really love people, you get excited about them and you want to help them. You get enthused about the projects that help people who are hurting, and this is what produces the energy. If you live right, love right, and pray right, God will get you so excited about some of the wonderful things to do in this world, that you'll begin to forget about yourself, and you'll think about others who have problems and rush in to try to help them. That's what gets you really turned on!

One day while I was in a board meeting, somebody said, "Why is it that some people have more energy than others?" And there was one negative-thinking person who spoke up and said, "It's all a matter of glands. Some people have energetic genes." And she pointed out that the endocrine glands are mostly responsible for rushing the adrenaline into the blood. I said, "But what stimulates the glands to activate the adrenaline?" Her answer led me to say, "Then actually, it's more a matter of the blands than of the glands."

> **Love is an energy-producing force.**
> **I will tune in to the source of love, today.**

A New Day for a New Heart

"For whoever will save his life will lose it, and whoever loses his life for my sake will find it."

Matthew 16:25

Some people are tired because they're afraid they're going to get tired. And because they're going to get tired, they don't spend their energy because they want to save it. And because they're not spending it—because they're saving it, they're constantly fatigued. If you don't have energy, the best way to get it is to give it out.

When I woke up this morning, it was still black outdoors. I had no idea what time it was. Then I heard our clock and I knew it was 5:00 a.m. "Boy, I'm still tired," I thought. I turned over to go back to sleep when I thought, "If I want energy, the best way to get it is not to spend another hour in bed, get your running suit on and take a long run." The truth is I didn't *want* to get out of bed. I was much too tired to run. But I had to prove to myself that my theory was right. I slowly donned my running suit and began slowly to jog down the street. The amazing thing is, that the more energy I spent, the more energetic I became. By the time I arrived home, the blood was coursing through my veins. I got energy by giving it out! Energy is inside of you! You have to prime the pump!

> **Energy produces energy.
> Get up and start—now!**

A New Day for a New Heart

"Happy is the man who listens to me, watching daily at my gates, waiting beside my doors, for he who finds me finds life . . . and gains favor from the Lord."

Proverbs 8:34,35

Recently I was asked to attend a board meeting at a corporation of which I am not a member of the board. The meeting was with a couple of high-powered realtors, a landowner, and the landowner's lawyer. Suddenly the lawyer became very upset. I was shocked. I could tell that if I stayed in that kind of negative climate, I'd be fatigued in a matter of minutes. The lawyer soon stormed out shortly after his outburst of temper.

I resumed when he left, but quickly reversed the emotional vibrations by suggesting some positive bait. Pretty soon we were all dreaming about the project that had brought us together originally. And as we dreamed, we became excited, which in turn made us more enthusiastic.

Do you want energy? Power comes through positive and negative wires. Gravitate to anything that will produce power to dream dreams and get involved in projects and get excited.

There are people who use an enormous amount of energy to resist God's Holy Spirit when He tries to move into their lives. And what happens? *God stays out and they stay tired!*

Pull away from negative forces and draw close to the positive spirit of Jesus Christ.

A New Day for a New Heart

"The Lord is my strength and my song."

Exodus 15:2

At the end of every day, the last thing I do is to have a prayer. "Father in Heaven, Jesus Christ, I've sinned again today." And I try to think of what my sins are specifically. I confess. I ask God to forgive me. I know He does. He died on the cross for me. And on the strength of His promise and power to forgive sins, I can put my head on the pillow every night without a feeling of guilt! I've asked for forgiveness and I know He gives it!

Now, that's the first thing I pray for. Then I pray for His Spirit to come and fill my life. I know He does, so I sleep very peacefully. If I wake up very, very early it's because I'm so enthused and excited about things I can do for God that I can't wait to get dressed and get to work. Then I begin the day with this prayer: "Father in Heaven, this morning is a brand new day! Filled with bright new opportunities!" Isn't that exciting!

If you begin your day that way and if you end your day that way, chances are that in between you're going to have a lot of positive emotions, because the Holy Spirit of God will come into your life, guide you, lead you, and direct you. You're going to get involved, and that means you're going to get excited, and it also means you'll become enthused! And that means energy!

> **I will live today as a new person because
> Jesus forgives me and gives me a new life,
> new love, and enthusiasm.**

A New Day for a Fresh Start

"I can do all things through Christ who strengthens me."
Philippians 4:13

Live right, love right, pray right, and think right. You'll be surprised at the energy output that is going to come out of your life.

Emerson said, "The world belongs to the energetic." And Sir Thomas Buxton said, "The longer I live, the more deeply I'm convinced that what makes the difference between one man and another is energy, that invincible determination, a purpose that once formed nothing can take away. This energetic quality will do anything that is meant by God to be done in this world, and no talent, no opportunity, no circumstances will make anyone without it."

Are you afraid to dream new dreams this year because you've dreamt before only to find your dreams lying broken around you? What was it that kept you from succeeding? Lack of determination? Lack of energy?

Whatever it was—you don't have to let the same weakness pull you down again. Pick a new dream for the new you. Tune in to God's Spirit. Is your dream His dream? Tune in to God's people—don't try to do it all alone. Get in touch with the Holy Spirit—to strengthen you and enliven you and help you become a new you!

> **I am not the same person I was yesterday, nor am I the person I will be tomorrow, I am always changing. Lord, direct the changes so that I shall be more like You!**

There Is a Miracle to Match Your Dream

A Miracle Every Day

"Righteousness will go before him, and make his footsteps a way."

Psalms 85:13

"A hundred million miracles are happening every day, but only those who have the faith will spot them on life's way."

It's really true! You and I will never know how many miracles God has performed in our lives until we meet Him in eternity.

Have you ever heard people make the following comments?

"An odd coincidence."

"I had a marvelous serendipity."

"A wonderful thing happened yesterday."

"You'll never guess who I ran into today."

"You'll never believe what I experienced."

"Boy, did I hit it lucky a little while ago."

"That's odd."

And so the world calls these happenings coincidences, serendipities, and unexpected good luck. But I call them acts of God or, in another word, *miracles!*

Reflect over the past few days or weeks. Can you identify miracles in your life? Write one or two incidents here.

1. _____

2. _____

**The miracle of believing
is mine today!**

A Miracle Every Day

"For great is thy steadfast love toward me; thou has delivered my soul from the depths of Sheol."

Psalms 86:13

Every week people all over the United States write me, "Dr. Schuller, I just happened to turn on the television set because I wanted to look at a football game, a movie, or some other program. As I was turning the dial, I stopped for a moment on your program and started listening.

"The odd thing is I've never been very religious. I don't go to church. I don't even claim to be a believer. But I listened to what you were saying. I tuned in the following Sunday and for several weeks after that. Today, I know God. He is real, and He's my closest Friend."

The world calls it chance. Positive-thinking people call it *God!* God working in our lives for our benefit and growth— miracles.

All miracles are designed to make your life beautiful. That's God's goal for you!

> **The miracle of God's steadfast love is mine!**

A Miracle Every Day

"Open my eyes that I may behold wondrous things out of thy law."

Psalms 119:18

I believe that every human being experiences many wonderful miracles every day. Unfortunately, some of us don't know it. We probably just don't know how to identify them, or perhaps we have an unrealistic definition of a miracle.

What is a miracle? A miracle is a beautiful act of God's providence moving into our lives. Something that happens which we can't explain and in which we had no control. All indications pointed to disaster, but it worked out actually better than planned.

God is good to each of us. If you don't see miracles happening in your life, it doesn't mean God isn't doing something good for you. It means you may not be spiritually capable of identifying His involvement in your life. We need to develop the skill of counting our miracles daily. In order to do this we must fully develop our ability to recognize a miracle.

> **I'll watch for God's everyday miracles in my life!**

A Miracle Every Day

"For every thing there is a season, and a time for every matter under heaven."

Ecclesiastes 3:1

Ann Fischer once shared how she survived Jewish extermination in the Second World War. She was the only survivor from a family of eight children. Meanwhile, the man she was engaged to before the whole outbreak occurred, an architectural student named Benno Fischer, was the only one of a family of ten children to survive the extermination. Both of them survived the holocaust, though *neither one was aware of the other's survival.* When Benno looked up an old friend in Munich, he learned that a friend's mother had survived and was living in Stuttgart, Germany. Benno said, "I will go with you to visit your mother. Since your father died in my arms in the concentration camp, I would like to tell your mother about the last moments of his life."

So they went to Stuttgart. After his mission was accomplished, Benno went to catch a bus to return to Poland, never again expecting to return to Germany.

At the bus stop he saw a woman who looked familiar. He paced back and forth. He could not believe his eyes. It must be someone who looked like the girl he was engaged to marry four years before. And then she, suspecting she was being stared at, turned around; and they fell into each other's arms. As Benno said, "It was a miracle of God. I had never been to Stuttgart before . . . or since."

> **God's miraculous timing for my life
> is perfect!**

A Miracle Every Day

"If you seek it like silver and search for it as for hidden treasure, then you will understand the fear of the Lord and find the knowledge of God."

Proverbs 2:4,5

Spotting a miracle is a lot like whale watching. Once a year the great California gray whales migrate from Alaska to Mexico to give birth in waters that approximate the female's womb.

Year after year I have practiced the art of whale watching. When I invite a friend to join me, very often the response I get is, "I don't see any whales out there."

How do you spot a whale? First, believe they're out there. Believe that there is life lurking and moving beneath the surface, even though you may not see it.

Second, don't look for something dramatic. Look for something quite natural, like an exceptional swirl on the surface of the water. Then watch for a puff of fog. Keep your eyes on it, and eventually you'll see a hump of black and maybe even a whole tail lift out of the water before it plummets down and disappears.

You look for miracles the way you look for whales. First you believe in God. Second, you focus on Him. Then you will see evidence that He is actively involved in your life.

**Father, open my eyes to see
Your miracles!**

A Miracle Every Day

"Keep your heart with all vigilance; for from it flow the springs of life."

Proverbs 4:23

Why don't we see the miracles that are happening all the time? Let me give you this example. Have you ever been hospitalized for a week or more? The day you were released, didn't it seem the flowers were bigger? The sky, bluer? The world, brighter? You had a tremendous, almost ethereal, dimension of awareness.

Here's another illustration. When you return from a vacation to the house you've lived in for years, it looks different. All the familiar rooms and belongings you see now in a way you didn't see them before. You experience heightened sensitivity in the area of human perception.

How can these experiences be explained? Quite simply. A blanket of daily, accumulated anxieties, fears, depressions, jealousies, problems, and difficulties was temporarily lifted. What blinds us to our brighter world? What blinds us to the miracles God is performing? It is our negative emotional attitude. It's the bad news we've just heard or the worse news we're expecting. If we allow ourselves to react negatively to life's daily problems to the point we are no longer able to spot the miracles happening all around us, we deny ourselves so much of the beauty God planned for us to enjoy.

Open the "miracle-spotting window" in your mind. Begin today to really look at the beauty around you and practice a new heightened awareness.

> God's power within me
> reveals beautiful miracles about me!

A Miracle Every Day

"Set your mind on things that are above, not on things that are on earth."

Colossians 3:2

There are miracles happening all the time. Why don't we recognize them? One reason is we are cybernetically and subconsciously so conditioned by negative vibrations in this impossibility-thinking society we live in that we become de-sensitized.

But there's another reason why we emphasize the bad instead of the good. It's because it feeds our negative emotions. You know the Bible teaches us that man is by nature conceived and born sinful. Now what does that mean? It means that by nature we are out of touch with God. And when we're out of touch with God, we look for the bad instead of the good. We become cynical, skeptical, and suspicious instead of trusting, hopeful, and believing. So in a sense, we hunger for bad news!

We need to get in touch with God to become expert miracle spotters. One way we can do this is by developing an appreciation for all that He has created. Do not limit this appreciation, however, to material things only. The twinkle in someone's eye, an understanding friend's smile, a child's laughter, or a tender voice inflection, together and separately, confirm our loving Creator's handiwork.

Count your miracles every day. Become an expert miracle spotter and experience joy every day of your life!

**God's everyday miracles
bring me joy!**

Meet the Miracle Maker

"I believe. Lord, help my unbelief."

Mark 9:24

Chance meetings, chance greetings, off-the-cuff remarks are today's miracles. This very moment God is trying to say something to you. And when God decides to move personally into your life and do something with you, that's a miracle.

But it takes two to make a miracle. Only you can start a miracle. Only God can finish it.

I read about two young boys who were raised in the home of an alcoholic father. As young men, they each went their own way. Years later, a psychologist who was analyzing what drunkenness does to children in the home searched out these two men. One had turned out to be like his father, a hopeless alcoholic. The other had turned out to be a teetotaler. The counselor asked the first man, "Why did you become an alcoholic?" And to the second, "Why did you become a teetotaler?" And they both gave the same identical answer in these words, "What else could you expect when you had a father like mine?"

It's not what happens to you in life but how you react to it that makes the difference. Every human being in the same situation has the possibilities of choosing how he will react, either negatively or positively.

I believe in miracles. But I know that it takes two to make a miracle . . . God and you. Become receptive to a closer relationship with God. Choose positive thoughts. Choose miracles. Choose God.

> **I choose to believe in
> God's daily miracles!**

Meet the Miracle Maker

"When he had brought out all his own, he goes before them, and the sheep follow him, for they know his voice."

John 10:4

How can you make a miracle in your life? Belief in God is where miracles begin.

A few years ago, Mrs. Schuller and I went on a cruise. One day on the ship, we heard over the intercom, in a beautiful Scandinavian accent, "This is your captain speaking." Since we had not yet met the captain, we didn't know what he looked like. But we *believed* we were hearing the captain's voice, and with due respect, all the passengers stopped their activities to hear the message. Even though we had never seen him, we *knew* it was the captain.

Human beings ride on a ship called planet earth that spins at an incredible rate, flying through the universe. And I have good news for you. There is a captain of that ship. He is Jesus Christ. He deserves our attention when He speaks. But we must develop our "listening capability" in order to hear Him. Even though you haven't seen Him or learned to hear Him, believe He's there! When you believe it, there will be an event, for belief is the first step needed to make a miracle happen. God makes miracles happen, but you must get started—by believing.

Practice "listening" to God's voice. Assume that Jesus is trying to speak to you. Be very still. Quiet your mind. Concentrate on His voice. Spend five minutes "listening" then write down the thoughts that entered your mind during this exercise.

God's positive plans for my life are learned by listening to Him.

Meet the Miracle Maker

"For in him, the whole fullness of deity dwells bodily."
Colossians 2:9

If you were an invisible god, how would you relate to visible? How can the spiritual relate to the material? How could you prove yourself, if you were an invisible god, to material human beings? Think about that for a moment.

There is only one way—you would have to make yourself visible. And that God did, once in human history. He came in the form of a baby called Jesus. He came to demonstrate that His heart was filled with love.

If you want a closer relationship with God, get close to Jesus. Don't listen to what traditions may say about Him. Pick up your Bible and read what Jesus has to say about Himself. Learn about the human characteristics He revealed.

Look up the following Scriptures and find out more about Him.

Compassion . . . . John 11:28–44
Dependence . . . . John 17
Obedience . . . . Luke 22:41,42
Fear . . . . .1 John 4:18
Love . . . . John 3:16,17

> **Knowing Jesus means**
> **growing to be like Him.**

Meet the Miracle Maker

"When Christ, who is our life, appears, then you also will ap-
pear with him in glory."

Colossians 3:4

How can we relate the perfection and sinless life of Jesus
to our own imperfect, sinful ones? If the wonderful characteristics He possesses are in Him, and we invite Jesus into
our hearts, then those same characteristics become a part of
us, too.

When you have a relationship with Jesus, you then discover how beautiful you can be because beautiful feelings
come inside of you.

In a conversation once a man said to me, "I don't know if
I'm living right with God." I replied, "I don't think you are
or you wouldn't have raised the question." "How do I get
close to God?" he asked. "Ask Him to come into your
heart," I responded. "That sounds too simple. I'm sorry, I
can't believe it's that simple," he said.

Well, it is that simple. It all begins by making friends with
Jesus Christ.

Let the beauty of Jesus
be seen in me.

Meet the Miracle Maker

"Jesus said to him, 'I am the way, and the truth, and the life; no one comes to the Father but by me.' "

John 14:6

The way to strengthen your belief in God is through faith. *Choose* to believe in Him, and some time, somehow, some way He will communicate to you through an intuition, emotion, concept, or belief. Faith is a three-pronged concept. It consists of knowledge, trust, and assent. Faith and belief in God is the combination that starts miracles.

Miracles cannot happen without faith. And faith only happens when you begin to cast yourself out on a great idea that is seemingly humanly impossible. That is what faith is. And the concept of God Eternal's coming to earth and living like a human being is a humanly impossible idea. But cast yourself out on that idea—and discover a miracle in your life.

Choose to believe in Him. Ask Him into your heart and life today.

Jesus, I'm learning about You. I sure don't have all the answers. No one does. But I *choose* You and want to have a closer relationship with You. Come into my heart, Lord, and begin Your work in my life.

> **I believe in the Miracle Maker,
> Jesus Christ.**

Meet the Miracle Maker

"Ever since the creation of the world, His invisible nature, namely, His eternal power and deity, has been clearly perceived in the things that have been made."

Romans 1:20

To understand God's miracles you have to understand that God has limited His own power. God's power is restrained first by the nature of nature.

When God built this world, He built into the universe natural laws, such as the law of gravity. God's power is therefore limited, but this is no indignity to His character. God's decision to restrain His power only glorifies Him more.

It is because God is holy that He restrains His power. Power restrained is power improved! Unrestrained power means there are no ethics. The person with power bulldozes or pushes his will on others. So, again, power restrained is power improved!

God has restrained His power by the nature of nature. No person will ever be able to jump off a building and on the way down say, "God, I'm going to test your power. Please let me fall and not get hurt." It doesn't work that way.

Nor could you cut off your arm and then look for the miracle that would grow it back. You'll be disappointed. It'll never happen.

God respects and honors the natural laws He created into His universe, and we must learn to respect and honor them also.

> **The Miracle Maker's power within me makes miracles possible.**

Meet the Miracle Maker

"I will strengthen you, I will help you. I will uphold you with my victorious right hand."

Isaiah 41:10

God's power is also restrained by the nature of man. He made you and me with a certain degree of free will. He wants persons, not puppets! He could have created every human so that we would be nothing more than brilliant computers responding to God who sits in heaven at the master control. No free will.

The nature of nature, the nature of man, and finally the nature of God, limit His power. God respects the dignity of persons in such a way that He will not overpower your will against your own decision to act.

If you decide that you want to do something without regard to the Ten Commandments, the Word of God, or the teachings of Jesus, God will let you have your way. He respects your independence. He will advise you. He will direct you. He will enlighten you. But it is ultimately your decision!

When my son was a little boy, he would drive our car at the empty drive-in church during the week. He would sit in my lap, his tiny hands on the wheel, and he'd skillfully manipulate the curves and park the car. Unknown to him, I would be holding the bottom of the wheel.

Only God knows how many times you were spared from a crisis because He kept His hand, unseen, at the bottom of the wheel.

**The strong arms of the Lord
uplift me!**

The Miracle of Self-Discovery

"The Lord will fulfil his purpose for me; thy steadfast love, O Lord, endures forever."

Psalms 138:8

If your life is going to be beautiful, you have to feel like you are a success within yourself as a person. Nothing will make your life feel more ugly than if you feel you're a failure. I've had my discipline in both psychology and theology. Through this study I've learned that nothing is more dangerous and destructive to the human personality than when a person believes he is a failure. So I believe success is a necessary part of a healthy person.

How do you succeed? You succeed by hook and by crook.

I fish once in a while, but there has never been a time when the fish jumped into my boat. I'm a great believer in positive thinking, but the fish will not just jump in! I have to try. I have to plan. I have to make the effort. First, I throw out the fish hook. The hook is I have to do all I can.

The staff of the Good Shepherd means that after I've done my best, I can trust God with it. If it's part of His plan, it will happen. That's the crook!

The hook and the crook are symbols of assured success that you can make it. You can be what God wants you to be, by hook and by crook.

God's steadfast love
stimulates my success!

The Miracle of Self-Discovery

"But thanks be to God, who in Christ always leads us in triumph, and through us spreads the fragrance of the knowledge of him everywhere."

2 Corinthians 2:14

Within every person's lifetime, God will create an opportunity for him to grow into the person He wants him to become.

A few years ago I went through the Museum of Atheism in Levov, Russia. I prayed, "O God, use me to say something to this Communist guide." I looked at her and said, "Before I say good-bye, I have good news for you." "What's that?" she asked. Watching her eyes very carefully for any reaction, I said, "God loves you, even if you don't believe it. You may be an atheist. You have that freedom. But that doesn't change God one bit. He still loves you, even if you don't believe it." She winced.

To this day I have felt it was one of those times in my life when an off-the-cuff comment prompted by the Holy Spirit burned its way into a consciousness and will never leave it. I dare believe with all my being that she was cybernetically tattooed with that concept. I have no doubt that someday she will become a believer and grow into the person God wants her to be.

There is a more beautiful you waiting to come through.

The fragrance of God's miraculous love
brings beauty to my world.

59

The Miracle of Self-Discovery

"So if the Son of Man makes you free, you will be free indeed."

John 8:36

There is no doubt that every person has yet to discover talent, ability, and potential within himself. What keeps us from discovering our full potential? First of all, for many people it's an emotional blockage that perhaps stems from some hurt, defeat, or rejection. Too many people have surrendered their future leadership to their past hurts, defeats, or rejections.

A sixty-three-year-old woman told me her story. "I was thirteen years old when I became an atheist. I had had a terrible experience, so bad I can't tell you about it. I heard about God in Sunday School, so I prayed to Him, but my problem got worse. I began to believe there was no God. I became an atheist and stayed that way all my life. My husband and I have been married forty-two years. He went to church, but I would never go with him.

"One Sunday while he was at church, I turned on the television and saw you. Something about you looked loving and you twinkled, so I kept watching. I heard you talk about Jesus and something inside me stirred. I couldn't put my hand or my mind on God, but I felt something inside warm up. It was wonderful. I changed then and there."

Fifty years as an atheist, and by discovering faith, she also discovered herself!

> **In Christ, I'm free to be me!**

The Miracle of Self-Discovery

". . . and he reworked it into another vessel as it seemed good to the potter."

Jeremiah 18:4

What kind of person are you? Are you a negative, impossibility-thinking obstructionist? For instance, we've all seen the sign, "Don't confuse me with the facts, I've already made up my mind."

Or are you a progressive, possibility-thinking person? Someone who can be characterized by the following principles?

The progressive person . .

. . . believes he needs to improve. He knows he has a blind spot. Are you willing to admit that like every other human being you, too, have some blind spots? The result of your being indoctrinated, brainwashed, or prejudiced in some of your attitudes and viewpoints?

. . . honestly seeks constructive criticism and correction. You will never improve and excel until you receive some helpful, constructive criticisms. Are you willing to take that attitude and welcome constructive comments from friends who really want to help you?

. . . makes deep changes that lead to personal improvement. He begins to hear and apply what people have been trying to tell him.

. . . admits publicly his shortcomings, failings, and mistakes. He utters the sentence that more than anything else marks him now as a maturing adult. He says, "You were right, and I was wrong."

This person is about to be changed at a very deep level.

> **Father, mold me and make me
> after Your will!**

The Miracle of Self-Discovery

"For we aim at what is honorable not only in the Lord's sight but also in the sight of men."

2 Corinthians 8:21

The progressive person becomes a new person, an open person, a free person. No longer does he try to give people professional hauteur, the pontifical pride melts away. Suddenly he stands there just another honest, humble human being.

"Maybe I am the head of the history department, but there are still some aspects of history I don't understand. I'm still learning."

"Maybe I'm the professor of theology at the seminary, but there are many things I don't understand."

"Even though I am the pastor of a church, I have my sins and shortcomings, too."

We're all trying to do the same thing, improve and grow into beautiful people through whom Jesus Christ can shine. So the progressive person becomes an honest person. No more masks. No more games. No phony claims. No false pretenses.

**Honesty and humility
enhance prosperity!**

The Miracle of Self-Discovery

"All this is from God, who reconciled us to himself and gave us the ministry of reconciliation."

2 Corinthians 5:18

God has a goal of turning everyone into a beautiful person. A bridge is built where there was no bridge. A wall is torn down where there was a barrier. Communication is restored; a fracture is mended. Polarization turns into dialogue. Suspicion gives way to trust.

The miracle of reconciliation begins. The one miracle that is better, greater, and more beautiful than all other miracles is reconciliation between man and God.

A progressive, honest person can lay himself wholly before Christ and open his mind for God's thoughts, ideas, and plans to flow through. He tunes in to God's personality and recharges his own with energy, enthusiasm, and purpose.

Reconciled to God, my life is recharged with eagerness to achieve miracles!

The Miracle of Self-Discovery

"A friend loves at all times and a brother is born for adversity."

Proverbs 17:17

In the early days of our ministry, a close friend of mine was the treasurer. He set the church up on a financial basis that is largely responsible for the degree of financial success we enjoy today.

After a few years, God gave us a bigger dream. He gave me the dream of a larger church on twenty acres of land. I knew it came from God, and I shared it with the people. Half of the people thought it was a great idea, and half of them were not so sure. I went to my office, and my friend's resignation was on my desk. It was a sad day for me.

Not long ago, I received a telephone call from my friend's wife. "John is very sick," she said. "His liver is so bad he's been in a coma twice. Now they're going to try a bypass operation around his liver. You know, he's always loved you, in spite of what happened. I thought if you'd pray for him, it would be great."

Right after we hung up, I called the Orange County Airport and reserved the only seat left on a plane leaving in one hour for Sacramento. In a rental car, I drove another hour to the hospital and found my friend's room. There he was sitting on the bed in a bathrobe. Now all 6'3" of him had dwindled down to 134 pounds. His eyes were sunken in his head, his cheeks were hollow. He stood up, walked over to me, and we hugged like two close brothers. We had a great time talking and praying together for two hours. Reconciliation!

**My road to happiness
is reconciliation!**

A Miracle of Love

"In him we live and move and have our being."

Acts 17:28

God made the universe in what we call ecological balance. That means plants, animals, fish, fowl, and human beings—all of us—need each other. And of all these creatures on planet earth, it was to the human being that God gave the most unique gift—the gift of faith, which makes miracles possible.

I'll never forget one time on an airplane I sat next to a medical doctor, Jewish by faith, who was trained in Poland. She was a great psychiatrist. I asked her, "Do you believe in God?" And she said, "Indeed I do." During our discussion I asked her, "What's the difference between man, animals, and the other higher primates?" She immediately came back with the answer, "While at medical school in Warsaw, my professor said, 'The difference between man and all other primates and animals is man has the capability of believing in God. And that's because when God created all kinds of life on planet earth, He wanted creatures to know that they were created by Him. So, He picked His highest form of creature, the human being, and gave him the revelation, the knowledge, and belief there was a God behind it all.' "

Through the human being, who alone is capable of believing in God, God fulfills His plans and His purposes by sharing creative ideas and setting beautiful plans in motion.

**God picked me for a
special plan and purpose!**

A Miracle of Love

". . . be not faithless, but believing."

John 20:27

Of all creatures on the earth, only human beings have the capability of being dreamers. We can think. We get ideas. And every miracle starts with an idea, which is a new beginning.

There are four important aspects to the miracle of a new beginning. A beginning is . . .

. . . simple. It starts with an idea.

. . . stimulating. It produces enthusiasm, energy, excitement.

. . . smart. It usually requires risk, but it's much smarter to start with risk than to keep living in indecision and thinking to yourself, *Some day, when everything's right, I'll do something about it.*

. . . successful. God put you in this world not to measure your achievement but to *mark your faith.*

When you start something, even though there's risk involved, and you can't be sure you'll make it, at least you're giving evidence that you've got faith. And when you do something that shows you have faith, *in that moment you are a success!*

**My fulfillment
is found in my faith.**

A Miracle of Love

*"Follow the pattern of the sound words which you have heard
from me in the faith and love which are in Christ Jesus."*
                                                    2 Timothy 1:13

One of the couples in our church realized they could not
have children. They prayed for a child, and one day the wife
told her doctor, "Maybe one of these days you'll hear of a
child who needs parents. If so, remember us." A short time
later, a miracle happened.

Their doctor found himself delivering a baby who was up
for adoption.

The excited parents thanked God and picked up their
new daughter.

Six months later they learned their daughter was stone
deaf. At the John Tracy Clinic, they struggled to teach her to
talk and understand their lips. Was she learning anything?
Was she hearing anything? Was she grasping anything? One
day the little girl had a very upsetting experience. Her little
world collapsed, and she burst into tears. Forgetting for a
moment she couldn't hear, the father looked at her and said,
as he had many times before with no response, "Come, give
Daddy a kiss." She looked at him a minute and then kissed
him! It was the first time he knew she had read his lips.

How do miracles happen? Ask God for an impossible idea
and give it all you've got.

Commit yourself to an idea that is humanly impossible,
then God can perform a miracle. Remember, an impossibility is nothing more than a big idea that hits a little mind.

**With God,
all things are possible!**

A Miracle of Love

"One thing have I asked of the Lord, that will I seek after; that I may dwell in the house of the Lord all the days of my life, to behold the beauty of the Lord."

Psalms 27:4

On a television program I saw, they were discussing the photography of Weston, now deceased, who was obviously one of the greatest photographers of our time. As the backdrop for the conversation they had one of his famous photographs. It was a beautiful sculptured mountain; in the foreground are three unadorned telephone poles. A novice would look at it and say it's a picture of three telephone poles in front of a hill. The truth is that it is a most unique, creative, dramatic, beautiful composition. As the panel was discussing the picture, the television interviewer asked, "Couldn't anybody take a camera, go out there, and take that same picture?" One of the critics said, "Nobody else could do it." "Why not?" asked the interviewer. The critic replied, "Nobody else would see it." And I think he's right.

I thought of that recently as I was driving down a canyon road. There in a ditch stood a young man with a camera, photographing what looked like just another dirty, old, scroungy, seedy weed. But he *saw* something maybe no one else would see.

God's beauty is about me
for the eye of my mind to behold!

A Miracle of Love

"You have not chosen me, but I have chosen you."

John 15:16

Do you believe that you are solely responsible for the shape your life has taken? Or is there, to some small or large degree, a destiny beyond your control that made and marked you for the person you are now?

A British scientist recently made a study that led to the statement that mankind is an organismic unity. "The nitrogen molecules that we inhale and exhale are spread," he said, "over the whole blanket of the earth's atmosphere every few years. This same air is constantly recycled so that we literally breathe the same air that Shakespeare breathed and the same air that Jesus breathed." He calculated that every person will breathe at least two molecules of the nitrogen that everybody else breathes.

We belong to a human family, and we are not the free-wheeling, free-swinging, independent people we think we are. From a genetic standpoint, some of the drives and modes, impulses and powers, that exist within us exist not because we chose them, not because we developed them, but because they were genetic to some degree.

**My life is the Lord's
for His leadership!**

A Miracle of Love

"When the Spirit of truth comes, He will guide you into all truth . . ."

John 16:13

Both Eric Berne and Freud taught that each of us has a parent-ego state that remains with us psychologically. We never totally shake off from ourselves our father and mother. But we can go beyond that. Your father had a mother and father; and your mother had a mother and father. Your grandparents had parents, and they all are coming out through you. If you go back only three generations, sixteen parents are inside you. If you go back ten generations, every person has within himself 1,024 parents. Twenty generations back you would count a total of 1,048,576 parents, grandparents, great-grandparents and great-great-grandparents. So, in effect, you might say that every person is like a giant 747 jet loaded with hundreds of parents, grandparents, and great-grandparents.

That explains some of the forces, some of the drives, and some of the genetic impulses that come through you in your lifetime.

The good news is there is a pilot for this jet. And He controls the destiny of the whole ship, including all of the ancestors that might be influencing it.

God in His guidance provides encounters, experiences, and other people that will give your life direction and purpose and has brought you to a great degree to where you are today.

**God's guidance
goes before me!**

A Miracle of Love

"Thou dost guide me with thy counsel, and afterward thou wilt receive me to glory."

Psalms 73:24

The Eternal God, God of your fathers and forefathers, has a plan for your life. And He is coming in contact with you in the form of ideas, persons, concepts, and beliefs.

Be receptive. This week you will run into people you never knew before. You'll think it's a chance encounter. But there will be an interchange, and you will be God's miracle in their lives. Or they will be God's miracle in your life.

You will cross into someone's life. You may never know how Christ will come out of your life—through a look, through a word, through a touch, but their lives will never be the same. God will use you to make a miracle happen.

Father, show me who You want to speak to through my life today.

It's Lent—Let's Eliminate Negative Thinking

Let's Add Faith

"Know therefore that the Lord your God is God, the faithful God who keeps covenant and steadfast love with those who love him and keep his commandments, to a thousand generations."

Deuteronomy 7:9

A few years ago, Mrs. Schuller and I boarded a huge 747 in Singapore. From the airport, it looked like a pretty nice day. As we took off and before the plane was at its full elevation, in the stage of flight when there was nothing the plane could do but climb, we suddenly ran into a terrible squall. It was a fierce storm. The 747 seemed to stall as it tried to plunge its way against a rainstorm. Tons of water slapped against the mammoth machine as it coughed and clawed its way through the tropical storm.

Suddenly the seatbelt lights went on and the captain said in a calm voice, "Everybody please be seated." Everyone complied, and as I looked around I saw total anxiety on the faces of all the people in the cabin. We made it safely over the China Sea via Thailand, and skirting over Vietnam, back home to Los Angeles.

I realized later what gave me confidence during that whole experience was the voice of the captain. He spoke calmly, firmly, and reassuringly. It reminded me that you and I need that same commanding voice as we head into the private storms of life. We can have that confidence when we have faith that God is in control.

> **Lord, be the pilot that guides
> and controls my life.**

Let's Add Faith

"He who has my commandments and keeps them, he it is who loves me, and he who loves me will be loved by my Father, and I will love him and manifest myself to him."

John 14:21

I heard an amusing story recently when I boarded a plane in Michigan and sat next to a man who was chuckling lightly. "What's so funny?" I asked him. "Well, the craziest thing just happened," he said, and then pointed across the aisle to where Ray Charles, the blind entertainer, was seated with his Seeing Eye dog. He explained, "The plane previously stopped at Detroit, and the captain came out and asked if there was anything he needed. Mr. Charles said, 'As a matter of fact, yes. Would you mind taking my dog out for a walk?' The captain agreed and took hold of the leather handle and led the dog outside. As the passengers waited nearby to board the plane, they could see the captain walking the Seeing Eye dog. Eventually the small audience watched the captain, led by the dog, head up the steps to board the plane. Right about this time the public announcement was made for all persons on the flight to board the plane. When the gate was opened, however, nobody dared get on board—not after seeing the captain led by the Seeing Eye dog! Finally the captain himself came out and explained, 'It's all right,' he reassured everyone, 'I have my sight!' Only then did everyone get on the flight!"

You have to know that there is a pilot in command.

> Lord, You are in command and
> that reassures my every step.

Let's Add Faith

"The Lord is in his holy temple, the Lord's throne is in heaven; his eyes behold, his eyelids test, the children of men."

Psalms 11:4

A lot of people claim to be agnostics or atheists and say there is no God. But the truth is they really aren't unbelievers.

Even people who call themselves atheists or agnostics still have in the back of their minds a nonverbalized assumption that something is in control. So the real question is not, "Is there a God?" but, "Is our belief in God pantheistic or theistic?"

Pantheism is a belief in a god who is a universal cosmic energy force. He is imminent in everything—a stick, a stone, very impersonal, and unable to relate to you. God the force does not have a brain, and therefore, the human being is more powerful than God. If God is only a cosmic energy hoax, a mixture of electrical impulses, then the god of pantheism offers no hope. The only hope we have is that there is a God who thinks and plans and is more intelligent than we are.

The truth is there is that hope! Theism is the belief in God, the Divine Commander—the pilot, the wise, creative, personal God! But does He share wisdom with us? Does He address himself to issues that really concern us personally—where the rubber touches the road, such as matters of love, sex, wealth, health, and money? Again and again the answer is yes.

I believe in the Divine Commander and have hope!

Let's Add Faith

". . . Now I know that the Lord will prosper me . . ."
Judges 17:13

God does speak to the needs you have in your life. Specifically, let's pick money. We all need it. We don't live in the kind of society where we're automatically taken care of. We can't ignore our need for it.

Our institutions need it—our colleges, seminaries, churches, and research centers all need it. People who complain that churches, for one, aren't doing their job need only close down every church, synagogue, and cathedral to see what a veritable hell it would be in this country. If you've never belonged to a religious institution, and you see all of the problems of crime, corruption, and immorality, and then point the finger at the obviously failing churches, my response is—"Don't complain if you're not involved and in touch with a well-intended institution. And believe—they need help too!

"Become a part of it. Give your heart to it. God has a solution to your money needs."

**Nobody has a money problem—
it's always an idea problem!**

Let's Add Faith

"We are God's work of art, created in Christ Jesus to live the good life as from the beginning he had meant us to live it."
Ephesians 2:10

The deepest need is the need for self-dignity, self-respect, and self-confidence.

What makes poverty so damnable and abysmal is what it does to the dignity of a person. The person who lives in abject poverty loses all self-respect. A human being who is born, bred, and raised in poverty is driven to become an animal. He ceases to recall his identity as a child of God! He ceases to be a person—and becomes a tool of political parties to be manipulated for a vote. He becomes an animal scratching for a crust of bread.

If we created the kind of society where you automatically send dollars to poor people, they would become enslaved to the extended hand. Whether it be the hand of a political party or religious institutions, the person has not restored his lost dignity.

God's solution to the problem is simple. He has created in every human being the capacity to be creative. His answer to the poverty problem is to give everyone the opportunity to develop faith and open up their minds to His ideas. God's solutions are always ideas! When you achieve solutions to your poverty problem through the development of your human potential that is in you because you're created in the image of God, then you solve the poverty problem through personal liberty and possibilities.

> **Lord, for You I'll reach my
> highest potential!**

Let's Add Faith

"And I will make them and the places round about my hill a blessing; and I will send down the showers in their season, they shall be showers of blessing."

Ezekiel 34:26

God speaks to the issue of money. Does He really care about your needs for it?

There is a poem that addresses this well:

> Said the Robin to the Sparrow,
> "I should really like to know
> Why these anxious human beings
> Rush around and worry so."
>
> Said the Sparrow to the Robin,
> "Oh, I think it must be
> That they have no heavenly Father
> Such as cares for you and me!"

**Barrels of blessings are mine
when I wait upon the Lord!**

Let's Add Faith

"For all the promises of God find their Yes in him. That is why we utter the Amen through him, to the glory of God."
                                                    2 Corinthians 1:20

The best thing God can give you is not a check, but creative thinking. Always these ideas will entail risk, always they will be frightening. If you respond in courage and faith, you shall emerge developing your human potential. God knows you need confidence overall, and only when there is the possibility of failure can you have the confidence that comes when you are following His guidance in faith. Not only will you rise out of poverty, but you'll be free from something far worse. You're free from the fear that would tempt you to surrender your freedom in exchange for a security check.

God doesn't want to see you in poverty. He wants to bless you. But He wants to do it in such a way that you shall have more dignity, more pride, and more freedom. God's whole system of economics is so simple. At the bottom line it is possibility thinking. And it comes down to one simple word—TRUST.

**Risk is the
back side of trust!**

Let's Add Faith

"Now as you excel in everything—in faith, in utterance, in knowledge, in all earnestness, and in your love for us—see that you excel in this gracious work also."

2 Corinthians 8:7

God teaches a very basic understandable law—one I rely on as much as the law of gravity. It is the Divine Law of Tithing. It is the law that whatever money comes to me I have to turn around and give 10 percent back to God. Why? If I give 10 percent to God, then I am showing my faith that He will give me the wisdom to make the 90 percent go farther than the whole 100 percent would have. When I do that and when you do that, God does not promise to make you wealthy or free from financial stress forevermore. But He does promise to give you ideas. God will give you opportunities, and it's up to you to make the most of them.

If your life is headed into a storm and you have financial problems, then come to the God who is at the helm. Let Him speak calmly, firmly, reassuringly to you. How will He do it? Through brilliant, risky, and challenging ideas. And God will not waste great ideas by giving them to you if you don't have the nerve to act on them.

Today, make a commitment to faith. Start to tithe. Commit yourself to give to God a tenth of what He gives you. I promise you the ideas will come into your life.

> The most powerful force in the world is a God-given idea that has been dropped into the mind of somebody who has the nerve to grab hold of it.

Let's Add Risk

"I know how to be abased, and how to abound; in any and all circumstances, I have learned the secret of facing plenty and hunger, abundance and want."

Philippians 4:12

Lent is the season of the year when we salute our Savior and focus on Jesus Christ. It is the time when we offer to Him our minds which can be channels for the flow of positive thoughts. Therefore, Lent in a positive-thinking church is a time for self-denial, a creative self-denial—eliminating negative thinking.

No one ever faced more stress and personal sacrifice with such a spirit as did our Lord. That's why we as Christians have chosen the cross as our symbol. It's a plus sign! Jesus taught us how to turn a minus into a plus. Jesus was the world's greatest possibility thinker. Lent misses the point completely when it becomes a negative self-flagellating, self-condemning, depressing trip. Yet aren't we supposed to deny ourselves? Isn't that what Lent is all about? Of course! But there is a positive and a negative way to deny ourselves.

Real positive self-denial is to deny yourself the comfort of living in a no-risk zone. Think about that! Real positive self-denial is to deny yourself the privilege of living so safely that there is no chance to living. When you deny yourself enough to be exposed to great goals and dreams that may bring criticism from those who don't understand you, or may be threatened by you, only then are you building something that will turn this world into a more beautiful place.

> **Self-affirmation is the beginning of self-denial!**

Let's Add Risk

"Jesus said to him, 'No one who puts his hand to the plow and looks back is fit for the kingdom of God.' "

Luke 9:62

I have sometimes been accused of not preaching the cross. My answer to that is simple. I preach the cross every time I motivate people to become possibility thinkers—for possibility thinking is the positive proclamation of the cross! When you become a possibility thinker, God gives you His plan for your life. When that happens, get set. You're going to have to live beyond your grasp. You're going to have to think big and daringly.

Too many people live in the totally protected risk-free life. It's like the story of the mountain climbers. One of the men slipped and fell off a cliff and landed on a ledge. He called out for help to his companions above him. "Both of my arms are broken, and both of my legs are broken!" he yelled. His friends hurried to help him and they threw down a rope. As they were pulling him up the cliff, someone shouted, "If your arms and legs are broken, how are you holding on?" The man cried back, "By my te-e-et-th!"

If you're hanging by your teeth, the answer is to eliminate negative thinking. You do that by following what I call The Ten Commandments for Possibility Thinking.

Over the next week, I will introduce these to you. If you will apply them, I believe you will experience a wonderful improvement in your life.

**Keep on
keeping on!**

Let's Add Risk

"Blessed are the pure in heart, for they shall see God."
                                                    Matthew 5:8

COMMANDMENT #1—Never reject an idea because you see something wrong with it.

There is something wrong with every good idea. Any time God gives you an idea, you can find some negative aspect to it. It's amazing how there are people who sit in a deliberating meeting and respond to an opportunity by finding fault with it. You don't throw away a suggestion when you see a problem. Instead, you isolate the problem from the possibility. You neutralize the negative. You exploit the possibility. Sublimate the negative. Don't ever let it kill the positive potential that is within the opportunity.

COMMANDMENT #2—Never reject a possibility because you won't get the credit!

God can do tremendous things through the person who doesn't care who gets the credit.

Don't worry about getting the credit. If you do, you'll become ego-involved in the decision-making moments of life. Decisions must never be based on ego needs. They must be based on other's needs and pressures that transcend your own desires. The reason this church is successful is because of the 1,500 laymen and laywomen who do all the work and remain the great unsung heroes.

> **Possibilities will thrive because**
> **God gets the credit.**

Let's Add Risk

"He who gets wisdom loves himself; he who keeps understanding will prosper."

Proverbs 19:8

COMMANDMENT #3—Never reject an idea because it's impossible.

Almost every great idea is impossible when it is first born. The greatest ideas today are yet impossible!

The important issue is whether the idea is a good one. Would it help people who are hurting? Would it be a great thing for our country and our world? If so, then develop a way to achieve what today is impossible.

Just because it's not possible today doesn't mean it can't be possible tomorrow. Our goals should always be based upon whether it would be a sensational thing to accomplish.

COMMANDMENT #4—Never reject a possibility because your mind is already made up!

I'm sure you've heard the saying, "Don't confuse me with the facts, my mind is already made up!" I've had to change my mind publicly more than once. People who never change their minds are either perfect or stubborn. I'm not perfect and neither are you. I'd rather change plans while still in port, then set sail and sink at sea.

Possibility thinking means
I'll let God lead the way!

Let's Add Risk

"Make me understand the ways of thy precepts, and I will meditate on thy wondrous works."

Psalms 119:27

COMMANDMENT #5—Never reject an idea because it's illegal! Read this carefully, or you'll misinterpret this one.

A good friend of mine acquired fourteen property lots to develop a twelve-acre commercial center. But he ran into a major problem. There was a flood-control channel. Never reject an idea because it's illegal. After all, they built the Prudential building over the railroad tracks in Chicago. Why can't we have a little water go under a building in Orange County? So he led a crusade and the law was changed. There are many laws on the book today that need to be changed.

COMMANDMENT #6—Never reject an idea because you don't have the money, manpower, muscle, or months to achieve it.

All it takes to accomplish the impossible is mind power, man power, money power, muscle power, and month power. If you don't have it, you can get it. Spend enough time, use enough energy, develop enough human resources, acquire enough financial capital, and you can do almost anything. Just because you don't have it—don't reject the idea. Make the commitment to do what's great, then solve the problems.

> **God's power makes His possibilities achievable!**

Let's Add Risk

"Therefore, behold, I will again do marvelous things with this people, wonderful and marvelous things."

Isaiah 29:14

COMMANDMENT #7—Never reject an idea because it's not your way of doing things.

Learn to accommodate. Prepare to expand. Plan to adjust. A different style, a new policy, a change in tradition—all are opportunities that need to be taken advantage of. Learn to compromise. Learn to be equilibristic. Maintain a balance between the tension of an opportunity that demands exploitation and the limitations of the resources available at the moment. Readjust your budget. Compromise your style. Accommodate your life-style.

COMMANDMENT #8—Never reject an idea because it will create conflict!

The longer I've studied possibility thinking, the more I've come to one conclusion. You can never develop a possibility without creating problems. You can never establish a goal without generating a new set of tensions. You can never make a commitment without producing some conflict. Every idea worth anything is bound to have some people who don't go along with it.

> **Conflict calls for**
> **Creative Commitment!**

Let's Add Risk

"Therefore do not throw away your confidence, which has a great reward."

Hebrews 10:35

COMMANDMENT #9—Never reject an idea because it might fail!

Every idea worth anything has failure potential within it. There is risk in everything. I don't think the United States needs anything more today than possibility thinking. The problem is with labor, management, and consumers. Consumers are told that if there is anything wrong with a product, don't buy it. If you do buy it, sue the company. Labor has its problems. Management has its problems. I don't think there is anything worse than the no-risk mentality we have in America.

If Jesus Christ had operated that way, He would never have died on the Cross. The whole principle of faith means you're prepared to make a supreme sacrifice for the greater good of others. There can be no assurance until it happens. Then you can't be assured it will last. Success is never certain, and failure is never final.

Success is never carved in granite. It is always molded in clay. You never reject an idea because there's some risk involved. You isolate the risk. You insulate the risk, and you believe you can eliminate it almost entirely.

**Jesus Christ's risk
insures my success!**

Let's Add Risk

"Commit your work to the Lord, and your plans will be established."

Proverbs 16:3

COMMANDMENT #10—Never reject an idea because it's sure to succeed!

There are people today who back off if they are sure they will succeed. One reason is because these persons begin to imagine the ego fulfillment this success would give, and with an excuse of being humble, they pull out. To all of my fellow Christians who are trying to follow Jesus, and say, "I should not try to be successful. I'm not trying for the top of the ladder. That's materialistic"—I must say, that's not true! To choose poverty instead of prosperity, failure instead of success, low achievement instead of top-of-the-ladder achievement simply for the sake of being humble is not super-Christian. It's dumb. Only successful people can help people who are failing. Only winners will survive to give food to the hungry.

That's the kind of attitude the world needs. LENT—Let's Eliminate Negative Thinking. If Christ is in your life, then be prepared to become a possibility thinker!

Possibility Thinking is an active faith in Jesus Christ!

Let's Add Prayer

"But truly God has listened; he has given heed to the voice of my prayer."

Psalms 66:19

On the telephone in my hotel room in Hong Kong was a little card which gave the area code of every significant city in the world. It had simple instructions to pick up the receiver, dial a specific number, dial another two digits, and then the desired telephone number to have direct connection with any private residence in any major city on planet earth. It's amazing.

Through satellite service, it is now possible to dial direct anywhere. That's exciting, for it is exactly like a sophisticated system God created thousands of years ago—a design that surpasses any computer or satellite system. It is a mode of communication that makes it possible to have contact between us and God simply by dialing direct. It's a system I believe in wholeheartedly, and one I want to share with you. It is the heart of true religion. It is the system of prayer.

**In Jesus Christ,
prayer is a local call!**

Let's Add Prayer

"Therefore I tell you, whatever you ask in prayer, believe that you receive it, and you will."

Mark 11:24

I read a story of a man who manufactured, canned, and sold anchovies through distributors. He and his partner made a mint. After one of the most profitable quarters they had, the distributor was so impressed that he tried them himself. He took one bite and nearly gagged. He called the manufacturer and said, "These anchovies are awful! They're selling like crazy, but they're horrible!" The owner said, "Well, you know, these anchovies aren't meant for eating—they're just for buying and selling."

There's a tremendous principle here—a great psychological truth. Many people don't really believe in their product. They don't package, market, or manage a product to meet a human need, but only to exploit a situation.

The same is true of prayer. There are people who approach prayer who really don't believe in its power. They merely play with it, not fully planning or developing it to use effectively in their daily lives. Praying isn't just for buying and selling. *Prayer is a tremendous spiritual force which harnesses natural spiritual laws.*

**Prayer is powerful when
I sincerely search for God's ideas.**

Let's Add Prayer

". . . I in them and thou in me, that they may become perfectly one, so that the world may know that thou hast sent me and hast loved them even as thou has loved me."

John 17:23

Jesus and his twelve disciples gathered around a table in a small, secluded room somewhere in the city of Jerusalem to celebrate the Passover. As was the custom, they broke bread and drank of the cup of wine, symbolizing the Passover lamb that was slain in their Jewish history back in Egypt. The bread stood for the body, and the wine, the blood.

Jesus held high the bread and said, "This bread is my body broken for you." Then taking the cup He said, "This cup is my blood shed for you." He looked around and said, "One of you will betray me. What you must do, traitor, do quickly." No one noticed Judas Iscariot steal quietly away to betray Jesus to the Roman soldiers.

The feast was finished with no one truly understanding Christ's prophetic words. A final prayer was given, and Jesus rose and led the eleven men to the Garden of Gethsemane.

Today let us think about what this scene means to us. Do you fully understand what Jesus was saying?

**Prayer is complete
communion with God.**

Let's Add Prayer

"If you abide in me and my words abide in you, ask whatever you will, and it shall be done for you."

John 15:7

Jesus reached the Garden of Gethsemane, stopped and said to His followers, "Wait here. I want to be alone, I must pray." He turned to enter the garden alone, except for Peter, James, and John, who began to join Him. "Wait here," He repeated, "watch and pray." And He slipped away as they dropped to the ground only to fall asleep in the late night hour. No one saw Jesus fall to His knees and pray the greatest prayer ever prayed:

"Abba, Father, all things are possible to you. Let this cup pass from me. Nevertheless, not my will but Thine be done."

This is the greatest prayer ever prayed, and within it are the dynamic principles that all true prayer must have.

**Lord, help me
to will Your will.**

Let's Add Prayer

"He was praying in a certain place, and when he ceased, one of his disciples said to him, 'Lord, teach us to pray.'"

Luke 11:1

Ask yourself these questions and see if your prayers pass this test:

1. Are your prayers truly loving?
2. Are your prayers truly believing?
3. Are your prayers truly honest?
4. Are your prayers truly unselfish?

Look closely at Christ's prayers as we deal with these questions.

"Abba, Father."—This is an affectionate Jewish phrase of the richest love held between a father and a son. True prayer begins in love.

"All things are possible to you."—True prayer is born in faith.

"Let this cup pass from me."—True prayer is totally honest.

"Not my will, but Thine be done."—True prayer is totally unselfish.

How do your prayers test by these four principles? If you apply them to prayer, you will see miracles happen!

```
Lord, guide me
into true prayer.
```

Let's Add Prayer

"We love, because he first loved us."

1 John 4:19

Are your prayers truly loving? It's amazing how many prayers do not rise out of love. They stem from hostility, resentment, jealousy, greed, or anxiety. Nothing can help your prayer life more than if you're truly loving God while you're in prayer. In turn you need to be truly believing that with God everything is possible.

Are your prayers truly out of faith? There's a profound psychological connection between the first two principles here. For if you truly have love, you'll be an incredible believer. Someone once asked me, "Where do you get so much faith?" And my answer was simple, "I love too much to doubt."

> **I love too much
> to doubt!**

Let's Add Prayer

"There is no fear in love, but perfect love casts out fear."
1 John 4:18

Faith isn't possible except in a loving situation. A person who is a cynic, an unbeliever, an atheist, or a doubter does not need more faith—he needs more love. Dr. Gerald Jampolsky, a remarkable psychiatrist, clued me into this: The two basic emotions in a human being are not love and hate, but love and fear. Fear is the presence of a lack of faith. The cynic may come across as very sophisticated, critical, and bright, but in truth, any psychiatrist knows that he is deprived of real love within. Only if you're truly loving can you become truly trusting.

Can you identify with these definitions? Think about ways you can become more loving to the people in your life. What can you do today to become more loving?

**Faith is the natural blossom
of someone who loves.**

96

Let's Add Prayer

"The Lord is near to all who call upon him, to all who call upon him in truth."

Psalms 145:18

If you're totally loving and totally trusting, then you can dare to be totally honest.

Are your prayers totally honest? Or are you playing games with God? Be honest with Him. If you're not truly loving, tell Him. Simply say, "God, I should be more loving and I'm not. Can you help me? God, I should have more faith, but I don't. Can you give it to me? God, let this cup pass from me. . . ."

Jesus was totally honest with God. He did not want to be crucified. He didn't want the pain. He had seen crucifixions as a boy. They were not swift painless deaths like our gas chambers today. He knew what was before Him, and He didn't want it. Yet He also knew that He was the bread to be broken, and the blood to be shed.

> **Lord, let my prayers reveal upright motives.**

Let's Add Prayer

"I can do nothing on my own authority; as I hear, I judge and my judgment is just, because I seek not my own will but the will of him who sent me."

John 5:30

Although He didn't desire to do His Father's will, Jesus knew that His only strength and nourishment came as He did God's will. "Thy will be done," He prayed. He was totally honest, and totally unselfish.

Are your prayers totally unselfish? If so, you've tapped into the power of true prayer. If your prayers pass these four questions, then your prayers will work miracles. *A miracle is when you discover God's dream and you have the courage to grab it even though you know you may be hurt or run into obstacles along the way.*

When Jesus Christ rose from His knees, He knew the dream God had for Him. He understood the plan and was prepared to pay the price. He was given the wisdom and courage to tackle it, regardless of the price. When you discover God's plan for your life and have the courage to do His will—that's a miracle!

> **Lord, show me Your will, then give me
> the courage to achieve it.**

Let's Add Style

"For God sent the Son into the world, not to condemn the world but that the world might be saved through him."
John 3:17

It may sound like an extreme generalization, but ultimately there are two kinds of persons—the optimist and the pessimist. Jesus is an optimist.

I heard the story of the optimist who tried to convert his neighbor, the pessimist. The optimist said, "Hey Joe, I just bought a new bird dog, a retriever. He is the best hunting dog ever bred." The negative-thinking neighbor pointed to the dog and said, "You mean that scroungy mutt?" The owner answered, "Come hunting with me tomorrow. I'll prove it." So they did. The optimist promptly shot two ducks which fell into a nearby pond. He then ordered his dog to retrieve them. Taking off, the dog headed straight to the pond and began walking on the water. He retrieved the ducks near the center of the pond and dropped them at the feet of his master. The proud optimist looked at his neighbor and said, "Did you ever see a bird dog do that?" The pessimist said, "No. But he can't swim, can he?"

Some people insist on being negative. They only look at the black side of life. Choose what you will be.

I choose optimism—
it breeds the good life.

Let's Add Style

"Let your light so shine before men, that they may see your good works and give glory to your Father who is in heaven."
                                                    Matthew 5:16

I had a conversation once with a man who told me that he had no religious faith, but he had heard a story about Jesus and wanted to share it with me. He also wanted me to answer two questions about the story. First, is it true? And second, if it is true, what does it say about Jesus? I agreed to answer his questions if I could and he told the following story.

"This guy told me that one day Jesus was walking along and came to this tree full of leaves. He looked for some fruit on it, but couldn't find any, so He cursed the tree. Two days later the tree was dead. Is that true?" "Yes," I replied. The guy shook his head and looked at me as if he had won an argument. "I don't know how you can believe in a guy like Jesus who would kill a tree."

"Jesus was teaching a universal principle," I said. "Style without substance won't survive! A gorgeous, wonderful show of leaves is a fantastic front, but the tree's purpose was to produce fruit. Big show—no substance."

> **Let my life
> reflect my faith.**

Let's Add Style

"Yes Lord, yet even the dogs eat the crumbs that fall from their Master's table." Jesus said, "Great is your faith."
                                                    Matthew 15:27,28

Some modern merchandisers who analyzed the market found out how many millions of dollars were being spent for dog food. They wanted to get into the market, so they hired the best merchandisers, marketers, and managers they could find to come up with a new brand of dog food. They then took their new product and advertised with television commercials, full-page ads in the leading periodicals and local newspapers until they blanketed the country. They set up a wholesale network and spent millions of dollars to kick off the product. However, after six months, they had done nothing but lose money. The manager called everyone together and reviewed their strategy. They had the best marketing tools. He said, "Why isn't the dog food selling?"

Finally, one salesman, a farmer from Iowa, stood up and said, "Pardon me, sir. It all looks good. But the problem is the dogs don't like it!" Ultimately, if the dogs don't like it, people won't buy it.

It is the same in your spiritual life—a principle for prayer. A pretty prayer package won't go far without the belief, or substance, to make it meaningful.

> **Lord, let my life reveal qualities
> that glorify You.**

Let's Add Style

"Neither is new wine put into old wineskins; if it is, the skins burst, and the wine is spilled, and the skins are destroyed; but new wine is put into fresh wineskins, and so both are preserved."

Matthew 9:17

A while back I met a man on a plane who manufactured a certain appliance. I happened to have his product. It was brand new when I bought it, but it broke six months later. When I told him this, the man said, "I'm sorry, actually they were designed to last three years." "Why three years?" I asked, "Why not five or even ten years?" He answered, "Because otherwise we wouldn't have as great a turnover. We have to sell new products every three years or we'll go out of business." I looked at the man and said, "Let me tell you something truthfully. A friend of mine just bought this appliance, but he bought one made in Japan. He believes it's a better quality and isn't going to fall apart right after the guarantee runs out."

Style without substance can't survive. Even in personal relationships, style alone can't survive. Sometimes advertisements leave the impression that if you're sophisticated, sexy, and smart, you'll get the guy or girl you want. In reality, only those relationships between two hearts that represent commitment and character will last through the storm of decades.

> **Lord, let my life reflect a quality commitment
> to You that will last forever.**

Let's Add Style

"Examine yourselves, to see whether you are holding to your faith. Test yourselves. Do you not realize that Jesus Christ is in you?"

2 Corinthians 13:5

The Gospel of St. Mark, Chapter 11, tells the story of Christ in the temple driving out the "religious leaders." He points out the Pharisees and says, "Oh, these Pharisees, how they love to pray standing in the synagogues and on the street corners so that they may be seen by men. They wear their robes, pray their eloquent prayers and practice their piety so that all might see how religious they are." Yet when a man fell by the wayside and called for help, these same Pharisees passed by and didn't offer a helping hand.

If you want your prayer life to be real, talk to God. Be open, honest, sincere, and frank. No matter how stylish, embellished, poetic, or beautiful your words are, unless your prayer has substance, it won't work.

Style without substance cannot survive, but *substance plus sincere style will succeed!* The secret to success is to find a need and fill it, find a hurt and heal it; whether it's in your prayer life, business, or relationships.

**Substance plus style
equals success.**

Let's Add Style

"And those who are wise shall shine like the brightness of the firmament; and those who turn many to righteousness, like the stars forever and ever."

Daniel 12:3

Success is taking your achievement and using it to help people who really need help. There are a lot of wealthy, successful business people who are criticized. But I know many of them who are committed to Jesus Christ. They know the secret of success. They know that real success is coming to the end of life and knowing that you were able to be a part of the solution, not part of the problem. Maybe it's helping kids addicted to heroin. Maybe it's reaching out to the poor. Maybe it's participating in a youth program. Whatever it is, you can be a success and use it to help others.

How do you truly get substance and style in your life? Through Jesus Christ. He teaches the principles that change everything. He will put genuine, caring love in your life. You won't be a phony. You'll really care about others. There will be substance to your character. And that will change your style. You'll be open and beautiful. Anyone becomes beautiful when Christ shines through. Substance plus style equals sparkling success!

**Substance plus style
equals *sparkling* success!**

Someday Is Today

Someday Is Salvation

"By grace you are saved through faith; and this is not of your own doing, it is the gift of God."

Ephesians 2:8

How are people saved?

It's amazing that many people think they are saved through human effort. They feel that if they join a church, practice religious ritual, and participate in the sacraments, that they will automatically be forgiven their sins.

But it just doesn't work that way. It's not just human effort that brings salvation; it's human efforts that find their roots in God and in Jesus Christ. Our salvation is a gift from God and our part is to accept the gift by believing in His Son, Jesus Christ.

**Thank You, Jesus,
for my salvation!**

Someday Is Salvation

"But to all who received him, who believed in His name he gave power to become the children of God."

John 1:12

There was a beautiful ship that was stranded in a storm on a sandbar. The gallant old pilot tried several times to push it off alone, but he failed. Then he got a bright idea. He waited until the next high tide. On the night of the highest tide, he took two friends with him and went up to the boat. When the water was at its highest, they all pushed and pushed. The *water* and the *push* dislodged the vessel, and it floated away free.

There are people who subscribe to our possibility thinking who believe possibility thinking is nothing more than human effort. Not so! A possibility thinker connects to the Greatest Possibility Thinker that ever lived, Jesus Christ, and looks to Him for power.

> **Today I'll let God's power
> make possibility thinking possible!**

Someday Is Salvation

"And we all with unveiled face, beholding the glory of the Lord, are being changed into his likeness from one degree of glory to another for this comes from the Lord who is the Spirit."

2 Corinthians 3:18

What does it mean to be saved?

It means not only to have eternal security but to be released from any obstacles or problems that keep us from developing into the full person God wants us to be. We are saved not only from something, but *for* something; from anxiety to hope, from fear to love, from shame to self-esteem.

List below five positive qualities about yourself, and your self-esteem will begin to flourish:

1. _____

2. _____

3. _____

4. _____

5. _____

**My salvation today means
self-esteem forever!**

Someday Is Inspired

"I am not ashamed of the Gospel, because it is the power of God for the salvation of everyone who believes...."

Romans 1:16

Twenty-five years ago when my wife and I came to this town to begin a church, I had the shocking revelation that the Baptists, Methodists, Lutherans, Roman Catholics, and Seventh-Day Adventists had established churches in this area. There was even a Jewish Synagogue. You name it they had it.

I was discouraged. It figured if every other church was here, who needed another church? I prayed about it and God gave me an exciting message. He said, "Schuller, fifty percent of the people who live in this community have turned all these churches and religions off. If there's anything that's true about your faith, you ought to be able to communicate it to them and they ought to turn it on...."

Nobody ever taught me in graduate school how to sell ideas to people who didn't believe in you; so I went back to school—on the sidewalks.

Fifty-four weeks and 3,500 doorbells later I learned a valuable lesson:

"Share the positive truth of Jesus Christ in a way that people will find *help and happiness* and the gospel of God's love has been truly communicated."

My discouragement vanished! As I watched others turn on to Jesus Christ, I became motivated to dream for God!

> **Love is love
> when I give it away!**

Someday Is Inspired

"May he give you the desires of your heart and make your plans succeed. We will shout for joy when you are victorious and will lift up our banners in the name of our God."

Psalms 20:4-5

"Is there anything I can do to help you?"

The answers I received to the question I asked as I went from doorbell to doorbell in the early days of this ministry brought inspiration for great plans for a great church.

"Do you have anything to help alcoholics?"

"*Someday* we will," I replied.

"We're not interested in religion, but our teenager has a problem with drugs. Can you help?"

"*Someday* we're going to have the best youth program in Southern California."

"We're having marital problems. Can you help?"

"My husband left and I'm alone. Do you have anything for singles?"

"We're not interested in church but my son has a good soprano voice. Do you have a boy choir?"

And on it went down the line. "No, but *someday* we will," I promised again and again.

SOMEDAY HAS COME! Today we have exciting programs for singles and young people, and counseling for alcoholics, drug addiction, and marital problems. Our Tower of Hope is filled with specialists to help people who are hurting.

FIND A NEED AND FILL IT! THAT'S THE MESSAGE OF JESUS CHRIST! And that's the success of the Gospel! That success can be yours!

**My eyes are open for needs
that I can fill with myself!**

Someday Is Inspired

"Woe to those who are wise in their own eyes, and clever in their own sight."

Isaiah 5:21

Two little boys went fishing and caught nothing. Discouraged, they decided to try again the next day. Again they caught nothing. Finally, on the third day, they caught a fish. Soon they were both pulling them in one after another.

"Hey, it's time to go home," one little fellow finally said to the other. "We'll come back again tomorrow now that we know where the fish are." And he began to carve an "X" in the bottom of the boat.

"What do you think you're doing?" the second kid asked.

"I'm making a mark so we'll know where to come back to," was the reply.

The second kid said, "That's dumb, we may not even get the same boat tomorrow."

As a fisherman, I learned years ago that you take your sightings by a mark on the shore and line it up with something on the opposite shoreline. Then you can find your place.

God's the point from which you get your bearing. If you build tomorrow on your own strength, you're writing your dreams on sand. You need a personal relationship with God where He hears your prayers and leads you to make the right decisions.

> **Today I'll dream God's dreams**
> **and succeed!**

Someday Is Inspired

"Let your light so shine before all, that they may see your good works and give Glory to your Father who is in heaven."

Matthew 5:15

Twenty-five years ago this church was born. And six years ago we dreamed of a cathedral that would let God's *light flow in.*

Today the building is filled with people caring for people.

We dared to dream God's dream of helping those who are hurting, and God made the dream a reality.

Reality is in the dream. When you dream, reality is in the opening stages. You don't see it or feel it, but the dream is the great reality.

List three ways you can help someone who is hurting today:

1. _____

2. _____

3. _____

**God, use me today to touch someone
with Your caring love!**

Someday Is Inspired

"I know the plans I have for you, plans for good and not for evil, to give you a future and a hope."

Jeremiah 29:11

IF YOU BELIEVE IN SOMEDAY, MANY DAYS ARE GOING TO BE GREAT DAYS!

There are some people who don't dare to believe in someday. If they can't get it now, they don't want to take a chance on it next week. They want to cut tomorrow out of the calendar.

Believe in someday, even if you can't believe in the present moment. If you believe in someday, it can literally keep you alive!

List below one goal for each of the next three months to begin building a successful someday:

April: _____

May: _____

June: _____

> **Today my plan is to**
> **succeed tomorrow!**

Someday Is Inspired

"But now, Lord, what do I look for? My hope is in you!"
Psalms 39:7

BELIEVE IN SOMEDAY!

This is very threatening to some people because at a profound subconscious level the very thought of hope is frightening. That's because there is an enormous antihope mentality in America today. There are people who are so skeptical and so cynical, that anybody who sells hope is a threat to them. Hope is a threatening thing to people who don't want to take the chance of getting hurt, especially if their dreams had turned to ashes.

Someday is a threat to the people who carve their dreams in the sand instead of carving them in the trunk of a tree. They put their confidence in the transitory instead of the eternal. When the next wave comes, their dream is washed away.

Put your *someday* in God's hands. He will inspire you with hope, then fortify you with confidence. He will see to it that your hopes find fulfillment.

> **My future is in God's Hands.**
> **I feel confident and uplifted!**

Someday Is Inspired

"Therefore, if anyone is in Christ, he is a new creation; the old has gone, the new has come."

2 Corinthians 5:17

Once when I was a child, I watched the fall come and the leaves turn into a glorious bouquet of red, purple, and yellow colors. Gradually they fell, one by one, to the ground until there were only a few left.

Finally, only one leaf was clinging to the bare tree. I watched that leaf every day and wondered how long it would still be there. I knew that when the winter winds came, they would blow it off.

The leaf would fall to the wind the way a lot of people fall to the negative approaches of change that manipulating parents or preachers use to get others to lose weight, join the church, study harder, or whatever. The negative winds would blow it off. But the winds came and the little leaf clung on. The tough blizzards came and the leaf clung on. Finally, when March came and the leaf was still on the tree something happened. That leaf heard someone say, "Let go." It was the tree itself. Let God put something beautiful in your place, a new leaf!

LET GOD PUT SOMETHING BEAUTIFUL IN YOUR LIFE. Let Christ come into your heart today and fill you with the newness of life.

He will inspire your somedays!

Today I let go and let God.
In Him, I'm new!

Trust God for Someday

"If you abide in me and my words abide in you, ask whatever you will and it shall be done for you."

John 15:7

After delivering a speech at a big convention hall, the gentleman who was to escort me to the hotel walked with me to the parking lot. He said the car was parked by the buses. Well, the buses had already left so the car was lost. After walking the two-acre parking lot, we finally found it. The driver breathed a sigh of relief and said, "Next time I'm going to park by the flagpole."

Until you are irrevocably committed to Jesus Christ, you are parked by the buses. You'll hear a voice here and an allurement there and a temptation here. Someone will say, "Come on, try it," and you'll follow because you won't be rooted down. There are people who are so free they are lost at sea.

There is a flagpole where you park your life. It is Jesus Christ.

This Easter Sunday, give your life to Him. Park at the flagpole.

He lived; that's a fact; and He died. But, He rose again. And this very moment He wants to come into your life.

When He does, your somedays will be eternal!

**My somedays
are forever!**

Trust God for Someday

"O Lord of hosts, blessed is the one who trusts in thee."
Psalms 40:4

I've developed a "Schuller Scale of Happiness." It's a scale of one to ten and is intended to assess responses to the question, "How are you?"

So answer the question, "How are you?" _____

_____

Rate yourself on the following scale:
1. Silence and tears.
2. Awful—stop the world and let me off.
3. Not too bad.
4. Pretty good.
5. Good.
6. Great.
7. Tremendous or terrific.
8. Fantastic.
9. Super.
10. Sensational.

My score is: _____

Today I will _____

to improve tomorrow and "someday's" mark on the Schuller Scale of Happiness.

> **I'm beginning to build
> sensational somedays!**

Trust God for Someday

"Happy are the people whose God is the Lord."

Psalms 144:15

In my worldwide travels I've often asked people the simple question, "How are you?" To some people, this question is just a way to open a conversation, but I always take the answer seriously.

The majority respond with, "Not too bad." A few say, "Oh, pretty good." Even fewer say, "Great."

When you trust Jesus Christ with your future somedays, you will raise your mark on the Scale of Happiness day by day. By this time next year you will see that your average has gone up.

EXPECT GOD TO GIVE YOU NUMBER 10 DAYS. (See Yesterday's "Scale of Happiness.")

> **Today I'm Number___and growing!**

Trust God for Someday

". . . CHOOSE this day whom you will serve . . . as for me and my house, we will serve the Lord."

Joshua 24:15

A lady recognized me on a plane and said, "Hello, Dr. Schuller." I said, "How are you?" and she could not respond. Her lips trembled and tears flowed. My heart went out to her because she was hurting. She was yearning for happiness.

At the core of every being is the desire to be happy. Happiness is a state of mind and is achieved by *choice*. You can be happy in any set of circumstances if you *choose* to be.

Your most powerful freedom is your God-given power of choice. When you choose happiness by trusting in Him, your somedays will be immersed in joy.

**Happiness is for today
and someday!**

Trust God for Someday

"Blessed are those whose strength is in thee, in whose heart are the highways to Zion."

Psalms 84:5

Virgil Fox, voted by his peers to be the greatest organist in America, believed the Crystal Cathedral needed the greatest pipe organ in the world. Stricken by terminal cancer, he still wanted to be the one to design an organ as beautiful as the building that would house it. He knew it would enrich the lives of millions for many, many years.

He studied the structure of the building with its acoustics and vibrations. He studied all the great organs of the centuries since Bach.

The organ that will continue to uplift and inspire people all over the world throughout the ages is this day being installed in the cathedral . . . BECAUSE ONE MAN DARED TO BELIEVE IN SOMEDAY! His belief literally kept him alive until he completed his dream.

SOMEDAY CAN KEEP YOU *ALIVE*—AND IT CAN MAKE YOU COME ALIVE!

> **Because I trust in God,
> I will succeed in every endeavor.**

Trust God for Someday

"And this is the confidence we have in him, that if we ask anything according to his will, he hears us."

1 John 5:14

Five years ago a wonderful girl I know was abandoned and divorced by her husband. She was so hurt by it all that she said, "Never again will I trust another man." As the years passed, she harbored the hurt and was not really loving life.

Then one day, after an inspiring church service, she found herself praying:

"O God, I *release* myself to you if that's what I need to make me enjoy life again. I'm willing to take a chance again."

God heard and responded to her heartfelt prayer. Five days later she met a wonderful Christian man at a dinner party. A deep love evolved and grew. I performed the wedding ceremony not long ago.

She *dared* to *trust God* for her *someday*!

What do you need to release to God today?

_____

_____

_____

_____

**Father, I release myself to You
and Your plan for my someday!**

Trust God for Someday

"One man gives freely, yet he grows all the richer...."
Proverbs 11:24

Some people don't dare to believe in someday because they're afraid of growing old. That's foolish.

I know a man who is eighty-two years old—the father of the bride I told you about yesterday. I sat next to him at the table after the wedding. He said, "This is the happiest day of my life."

I asked him what he did to keep busy and to be so happy. He said, "I have a garden, an acre of vegetables. Every morning I pick vegetables and deliver them to the poor people in town."

He's living on a number-ten scale! He plants a garden because he trusts God for someday!

Jesus Christ makes his life sensational!

**Each year I'm more enthusiastic
about life!**

Believe in Someday

"For we walk by faith, not by sight."

2 Corinthians 5:7

A print-o-matic is the first thing I bought for my church. Twenty-five years ago it was $60.00. It's a mimeograph machine designed to print what was then called penny postcards.

When I was ringing doorbells, each time I got a positive response, I'd add the name to my mailing list. Each week I sent out cards that said, "We've got an exciting thing happening at the drive-in church this week."

My mailing list grew and my congregation slowly built as they kept getting this weekly reminder.

The point is this: If you're a possibility thinker, you can start with almost nothing. You need to believe that you can start from nothing and go to the top.

When you start with nothing and set goals, you'll find yourself climbing the ladder of success and happiness.

**Strong faith builds
successful somedays!**

Believe in Someday

". . . We exhort you . . . to aspire to live quietly, to mind your own affairs, and to work with your hands. . . ."

1 Thessalonians 4:11

DON'T LUXURIATE!

The secret of success is W-O-R-K. When I ran the mimeograph machine and worked hard to get members, somebody said to me, "You'd better be careful, Reverend Schuller. You're kind of an ambitious young guy and you're working pretty hard. You've got to do something to relax."

So I was talked into learning to play golf. And I kept at it until it threatened my religion! Seriously, my problem with golf was I could never enjoy it unless I became better at it than I was.

I decided not to luxuriate on a golf course but to keep plugging away at the church with all I had in me.

List three luxuries that interfere with your success:

1. _____

2. _____

3. _____

**Worthwhile work
wins victories!**

Believe in Someday

"What does it profit, my friends, if a person says he has faith, but has not works?"

James 2:14

DON'T VEGETATE!

Soren Kierkegaard tells a story of geese that were flying to the safety of a warm climate. They rested at a farmer's yard to eat their fill of corn. The geese took off promptly to stay ahead of the freezing winds. But one gander stayed behind to eat more corn. His intended one-day layover extended to two weeks. Then, when he felt the biting cold raindrops on the tops of his feathers, he knew it was time to hurry on.

He ran as fast as he could with his waddling feet and wobbly body. He beat his wings for all he was worth but he could not get off the ground. HE WAS TOO FAT TO FLY.

The principle is that when you vegetate you become too fat to fly. You can go anywhere or you can achieve the impossible but not by vegetating!

Do it now!

Believe in Someday

". . . being no hearer that forgets, but a doer that acts, he shall be blessed in his doing."

James 1:25

DON'T PROCRASTINATE!

I took a walk on the cobblestone streets of Stockholm, Sweden at about 11:00 P.M. It was really too late to be out alone.

Suddenly I heard the rustle of feet behind me and I turned to see a gang of guys running after me through the darkness. I found myself encircled by them as I backed up against a wall. I was alone and figured they were going to hold me up. One boy spoke English and threateningly said, "Who are you and what are you doing here?"

I said, "My name is Robert Schuller and I'm from California. I'm just taking a walk."

Then the boy asked, "What do you do?"

I said, "I'm a minister of the Gospel of Jesus Christ. Do you believe in God?"

The young guy turned and threw the question out to the others and they all laughed. Then he said, "No, we're too young to believe in God. Religion is only for old men and women before they die. Young people don't have time for God. We have time for fun."

Faith in Jesus Christ is for everyone. You need it not only for eternity but to make the most of today.

> I've but one life to live.
> God's helping me live it to the fullest!

Believe in Someday

"Say to wisdom, 'You are my sister,' and call insight your intimate friend."

Proverbs 7:4

DON'T NEGATIVATE—POSSIBILITIZE!

To negativate is to take anything that has a potentially positive possibility and drown it with negative thoughts until it no longer holds any possibilities.

Don't look for the negatives in a given situation. Look for the possibilities.

Briefly describe a circumstance you are facing today:

_____

_____

What opportunities for possibilitizing do you see?

_____

_____

_____

**Keep on
possibilitizing!**

Believe in Someday

"Let us press on to know the Lord, his going forth is as sure as the dawn."

Hosea 6:3

DEDICATE!

A little boy, age six, was struck by a car and severely injured. Hospital bills continued to mount as months went by—over $30,000. The boy heard his mother crying over the bills.

"Don't worry," he promised, "I'll pay off the bills."

He collected papers, cans, and bottles for five years or so. A few weeks ago, he carried a check for $17,000 to the hospital with a promise the balance would be forthcoming.

DEDICATING means pray it through, give it all you've got. Be willing to start at the bottom and keep going up. Never quit!

> **Inch by inch
> my goal's a cinch!**

Believe in Someday

"Take delight in the Lord, and He will give you the desires of your heart."

Psalms 37:4

God has a beautiful plan for your life!

It starts when you are in tune with Him. You can't do it alone. It starts when you seek His guidance and pray for His direction.

Ideas will flow through your mind and God will flow through ideas. Emotions will surge through you and God glows through positive emotions.

Ask God in your quiet prayer time for His ideas. Listen carefully, then list the ideas below.

_____

_____

_____

_____

**Father, show me Your dream
for my tomorrows!**

Someday Is Possible

"Jesus stood up and proclaimed, "If anyone thirsts, let him come to me and drink."

John 7:37

In the next few days, I'll ask you some questions that will determine whether you are a possibility thinker or an impossibility thinker.

Today's question: Is it possible to drink sweet water out of the ocean?

For the possibility thinker, the answer is yes! I was once on a cruise in the salty Arctic Circle when the captain said we could dip down and drink water right outside the ship. We were in a stream of fresh spring water flowing from a melting iceberg.

A possibility thinker is somebody who believes that things are possible even when they can't be understood. That's why they believe in God!

> **Yes! I believe in the
> divine affirmative!**

Someday Is Possible

"Indeed the water I give him will become in him a spring of living water welling up to eternal life."

John 4:14

Here's another question:

Is it possible for water not to freeze when the temperature is always subzero?

Again, the answer is yes. At the high Arctic Circle there are lakes and rivers that never freeze. It's possible because they are salt water.

It's incredible how we all carry over our presuppositions into a situation. We prejudge and declare that something is impossible because we do not comprehend it or we have never experienced it.

Some people don't believe in God because they've never experienced Him in their lives. Therefore, they autocratically declare Him a nonreality.

Possibility thinkers not only believe in God, they are believers in prayer and in Jesus Christ. The core of possibility thinking is an abiding faith in Him.

> **God is real!**
> **I feel Him in my soul!**

Someday Is Possible

*"But for you who revere my name, the sun of righteousness will
rise with healing in his wings."*

Malachi 4:2

One more question:

If you miss the sunset, is it possible to get an instant re-
play?

Yes, to a possibility thinker!

I remember the time when we were to take the Concorde
from Paris to Washington, D.C. I was looking forward to
seeing the sunset from such an immense altitude. But there
was a delay and the plane took off late in the evening, about
10:00 P.M.

When we finally took off like a bullet into the blackness,
the sun had long set and the stars were twinkling brightly.
Soon we were traveling faster than the sun.

Suddenly the stars grew dim and the west began to light
up like a dawning. In fact, the west turned from the dark
evening into a glorious sunrise.

We literally caught up with the sun! I couldn't believe we
were seeing a sunrise in the west.

It's amazing how many things we say are impossible,
when they are really possible!

We have to release ourselves from our negative precon-
ceptions and release ourselves to God and His positive attitude of possibility thinking!

I believe it's possible!

Someday Is Possible

"Not that we are sufficient of ourselves to claim anything as coming from us; our sufficiency is from God."
                                            2 Corinthians 3:5

Just as God had a plan for Moses' life as related in today's scripture reading, He also has a plan for you.

He will meet your feelings of inadequacy with His divine power and make you *more* than adequate. He will lead you on to reach your highest potential.

God has a dream for your life. Become a possibility thinker and you will rise higher up the ladder and live a happier life.

Write down what you think God's dream for your someday is:

_____

_____

_____

_____

**Someday's happiness is today's
possibility thinking!**

Someday Is Possible

"Let us not become weary in doing good, for at the proper time we will reap a harvest if we do not give up."

Galatians 6:9

BELIEVE IN TOMORROW!

There are a lot of people who only believe in *now*. They are people who wouldn't plant a cypress tree because it takes too long to grow.

We have rimmed our property with cypress trees. Why? Because years ago I visited Villa d' Este on Lake Como in Italy and rested a few days among the most magnificent Italian cypresses. They were planted by Napoleon Bonaparte and now stand one hundred feet tall and twenty-five feet thick.

At that time I believed that someday this property would be ringed with a wall of green cypress trees almost as high as the Tower of Hope. So we planted cypress trees and someday, sooner than we think, they will be as tall as the tower.

Some people only plant petunias. They want to see the bloom now. They haven't learned to wait.

Today I'm making an appeal to you; DON'T CUT TOMORROW OUT OF YOUR CALENDAR! BELIEVE IN SOMEDAY.

**I will reap tomorrow's harvest
when the time is right!**

Someday Is Possible—Someday Is Today!

"Behold, this is the acceptable time. Now is the day of salvation."

2 Corinthians 6:2

I want to give you a sentence that sums up what we have been saying this past month:

TODAY IS THE SOMEDAY YOU WERE PRAYING FOR YESTERDAY!

SOMEDAY IS TODAY! Someday I'm going to break this habit. What is it? Smoking, drinking too much, narcotics? Maybe in the back of your mind you have said, "Someday I'll dare to fall in love again." SOMEDAY IS TODAY!

Someday I may even consider accepting Jesus Christ as my Savior. I will join a church someday. Let me tell you . . . SOMEDAY IS TODAY!

Do you know that if you don't believe in someday, you really can't live? HOPE is what keeps a person alive.

NEVER PUT OFF FOR TOMORROW WHAT YOU CAN DO TODAY.

Do you know God? Have you accepted Jesus Christ? SOMEDAY IS NOW!

> The acceptable time for me to
> plan for someday is now!

Chains or Change

Change Your Heart

"O sing to the Lord a new song."

Psalms 33:3

The beginning of a new life is to decide you are going to sing a new song. That means you have to make a new recording and get rid of some of the old records of your mind.

We all have a great collection of subconscious tape recordings. There are a lot of negative records in your life and mine that we have yet to discover and destroy.

I saw an ad in the newspaper advertising a huge piece of earth-moving equipment, and the bold words read "TURN-AROUND POWER." Built into that huge machine was turnaround power.

For a quarter of a century I have been a pastor and I've counseled with people, young and old, in every conceivable situation, yet I have never met a person in whom God did not build turnaround power. You might not have discovered it yet, but I believe God will help you identify it and *your life will be turned around!*

Since you have only one life to live, give yourself a chance to live right. Use your God-given, built-in turnaround power to destroy the old negative tapes and record some new songs!

> **Lord, use Your power
> to turn my life around!**

Change Your Heart

"All scripture is inspired by God and profitable for teaching, for reproof, for correction, and for training in righteousness, that the man of God may be complete, equipped for every good work."

2 Timothy 3:16,17

Some of the old records in your brain are very dangerous to you. You need to discover them and destroy them. Maybe the record you hear is one of the following:

"I can't break this or that habit."

"I don't think I'll succeed if I take that new position."

"I always try and fail."

"How can there be a God with all the evil in the world?"

"Christians are all a bunch of hypocrites."

All of these are negative, cynical records.

Examine your conscience and ask Jesus to help you handle your negative emotions.

These old negatives in your mind are dark corners. They are not illuminating you. They're not enlightening you. So, run to the Light. The Light where you will be illuminated, inspired, and enlightened—the Word of God. Spend at least ten minutes in the Bible this week, and increase it to fifteen next week. Each week increase the time by five minutes until you are spending an hour a day in your Bible. Notice how your life is changing as you spend more time in the Word of God.

> **Father, I'm eager to read Your Word, and learn more about You!**

Change Your Heart

*"I will instruct you and teach you the way you should go; I will
counsel you with my eye upon you."*

Psalms 32:8

One morning before dawn I went out for a long run. I
reached an intersecting point where I would have to either
keep on going east or turn to the south or north. If I turned
south I would have, with the breaking of the dawn, a view of
the ocean. If I turned north I would view the mountains in
the breaking sunlight. Both options were tempting. But if I
kept running east, I would follow what was a crowning,
golden glow; I knew I would catch the daybreak, and I
would feel the first long shafts of golden sunlight falling on
my chilly cheeks and cold forehead. There had been times
when at that same intersection I turned to run to the ocean
or mountains, but I ended up running with my back to the
daybreak. That was disappointing. I felt I was missing something beautiful. So I ran to the sunrise! When I reached the
top of the hill, the sun hit my face, the bursting light and
glory was like being born again.

It's like that with Jesus Christ. When we turn our lives
over to Him, His light makes us become born again. Jesus
Christ is the Light of the world. Choose Him as your direction and run to Him.

> **Lord, guide me and keep me
> daily in Your light.**

Change Your Heart

"Thy word is a lamp to my feet and a light to my path."
Psalms 119:105

The Bible is the wisest book ever written. There is unity in truth. A truth is a truth is a truth. You can't say it is a psychological truth and not a biblical truth. If it is a biblical truth and it relates to human nature, it is a psychological truth. And if there is a psychological truth about human nature, you can be positive that it is in the Bible. Perhaps the psychologists haven't found it yet, but it's there.

Good-bye and hello are two words that will help break the old negative records of cynicism, doubt, anger, hate, suspicion, distrust, and unbelief. All of these are negative emotions. When these negative emotions come at you and you are tempted to react the way you have in the past, say to yourself, "Here I am doubting again," or "Here I am listening to my unbelief again." And say good-bye to an old life and hello to new emotions of faith, belief, and love.

This transformation may require an act of God. But this is also where salvation comes in. The Bible speaks of a person being born again! It really happens. You can become a new creature if you will let your heart soften and receive the love of Jesus Christ.

> **Hello, Lord. Hello, Faith.**
> **Hello, Love.**

Change Your Heart

"And they shall turn their swords into plowshares."

Isaiah 2:4

Many people call these troubled times. Some say they are economically troubled times. And one can build a case for it. Others say these are troubled times because everyone is living under more stress.

If you have a battle going on inside, you can turn that problem into a possibility. Or, as today's Scripture tells us, "the sword can become a plowshare." The enemy can become a friend. The obstacle can become an opportunity!

While traveling through the Middle East, a pastor saw a young Arab boy playing on a flute making beautiful music. When the man, J. Wallace Hamilton, went up to the lad, remarking that it was an interesting flute, he discovered it was an old abandoned army rifle barrel that had been drilled with little holes. An instrument of destruction had been turned into an instrument of music . . . swords into plowshares.

God can turn negative-thinking, capability-limited human beings into positive, productive people if we will let Him.

> Lord, use my troubles to bring
> beautiful harmony to my life.

Change Your Heart

". . . to give them a garland instead of ashes."

Isaiah 61:3

I have on my desk a little bottle filled with ash of Mount St. Helen's eruption. I don't know if you've seen or touched the ash, but it's a mysterious product. A one hundred fifty mile area was leveled by the volcano, and the tragedy is, dozens of people lost their lives. But no negative is so negative that God in His providence can't turn it into a positive. And the positive results of the blowout of Mount St. Helens have yet to be measured.

In human terms, we cannot measure them. In commercial terms, we cannot measure them. But the sword can be turned into a plowshare; and in fact, that is what's happening right now. In time the land covered with ash will prove to be the most fruitful, productive land possible because of all the minerals in the ash. A whole new energy-generating concept is being developed from the heat in the soil. Possibility thinkers have moved in—not to exploit a tragedy, but to somehow turn a negative into a positive.

No matter what happens, God can bring good from every act, however tragic it seems. We just need to be receptive to His working in our hearts.

> **Lord, shine Your light on every problem I have, and show me its beauty!**

Change Your Heart

". . . that your faith might not rest in the wisdom of men but in the power of God."

1 Corinthians 2:5

A song that was popular years ago had a line which offered some good advice, "Accentuate the positive and eliminate the negative."

Since we are bombarded by negative thoughts and negative news, how can we eliminate them? Dr. Norman Vincent Peale said that every morning when you shampoo your hair, ask God to wash all of the negative thoughts out of your brain. We must do it constantly.

A few years ago, I witnessed a native in Thailand milking the poison from a cobra, and the scene came back to my mind. It was incredible how this native would taunt and tease the cobra until the head went up and the snake began to hiss and throw himself to strike the man with deadly poison. But the native was too clever. He knew exactly how to grab it at the back of the neck and squeeze under its jaws. First the mouth opened and the two ivory fangs were bared, then he would press the glands and the drops of white liquid poison would ooze out into a small vial. The cobra was milked to produce antivenom. Again a negative becomes a positive.

The native told me through an interpreter that three hours after he'd milked the cobra, the cobra would have venom again, enough to kill someone. It is the same with negative thoughts. You and I have to milk the cobra of our minds constantly.

Lord, replace the negative thoughts in my mind with Your positive wisdom.

Change Your Moods

"He who rules his spirit is better than he who takes a city."
Proverbs 16:32

Once on a trip back East to deliver a lecture on a college campus in Minneapolis, the plane put down in a blizzard that night, but the next day the sun was bright and beautiful and the golden sunshine was beginning to melt the snow at noonday. Somebody greeted me at the door of the lecture hall where I was to speak and asked me, "Did you bring this weather with you?"

I'm sure you've been asked that question yourself. I've thought a lot about it, and I've had this revelation: *We all bring weather with us wherever we go.* You always bring a mental climate, no matter where you travel. You step into a room, you meet people, you talk, and you either bring sunshine or gloom, shadow or sparkling enjoyment. You create a mood wherever you go. That mood you create and produce is a mental climate that others live with.

You must manage your moods or your moods will manage you. And over the next week I will present eight points that I believe will be helpful to you in managing your moods.

I'll spread the Lord's sunshine
wherever I go.

Change Your Moods

"Create in me a clean heart, O God, and put a new and right spirit within me."

Psalms 51:10

1. *Determine to manage your moods.*

Do not look upon the moods that come to you as something out of your control—something you can't handle. You are far more powerful than the mood that comes to you. It says very distinctly in the Scriptures that you can rule your spirit. You do not need to let your spirit rule you.

I remember a professor in seminary who said to us when we were studying for the ministry, "You will probably discover that there are some days when you are not at high peak. You probably simply need to withdraw and you can manage your mood by withdrawing from people for a while. After all, Jesus did that."

There was a time when the crowd pressed Him, and to handle His own mood, Jesus withdrew and went into the mountains to be alone to pray.

When you begin to feel out of control of yourself or a situation around you, get away from it. Be alone for a while. Sort out your feelings and then pray. Renew your mind and refresh your spirit in contact with Jesus, then attack the problem with a clear mind and a positive approach.

Renew a positive mood
within me.

Change Your Moods

*"For lo, the winter is past, the rain is over and gone. The flow-
ers appear on the earth, the time of singing has come, and the
voice of the turtledove is heard in our land."*
                                        Song of Solomon 2:11,12

2. *Get acquainted with your cycles and seasons and do not
be afraid of them.*

There are seasons in life and there are seasons of the
soul—the springtime when faith is born; the summer when
faith matures; the reaping and harvesting in the fall; and the
dark time, the winter, when you walk over frozen ground
and you're sure nothing will ever grow again. I don't know
of a single Christian who, in his pilgrimage, could testify
that his faith enjoyed springtime always. Everyone has the
wintertime of the soul.

Get acquainted with your emotional cycles. Make no decisions in a low time. Make no commitments in a low season. When you're in winter, be calm, be quiet and wait. The
mood of strength will return!

The low times that come are generally very natural, very
providential. They are planned for you to calm down, slow
down, refill, rethink, regroup, realign, get a new perspective,
take another check of your values, recheck your goals, and
before you know it, winter is passed. Spring returns with a
new aspect of your faith reborn.

> **Summer, winter, spring, and fall,**
> **God is in control of all.**

Change Your Moods

"Do not be deceived, for whatever a man sows, that he will also reap."

Galatians 6:7

3. *Accept personal responsibility for your moods.*

Once there was a little boy who was strongly admonished and rebuked by his mother. In a moment of anger, he yelled at her, "I hate you." He ran out of the house and into the woods, stood on a hill, and shouted into the forest, "I hate you! I hate you! I hate you!" Then he heard a voice (his echo) coming back at him, a stranger out of the woods, saying, "I hate you! I hate you! I hate you!" That scared him. He ran back to his mother and said, "Mother, there is a mean man in the woods. He's out there calling, 'I hate you.'" His mother said, "Just a minute, son." She took him back to the hill and said, "Shout as loud as you can into the woods, 'I love you! I love you! I love you!'" So he did. And the voice came back, "I love you! I love you! I love you!" "So," the mother said, "it is in life. Life treats you the way you treat life. Life is an echo."

Most of the moods we experience occur because of our own activity or lack of it. You and I are responsible for our moods.

I'll give God control of my moods
and always be positive and uplifted.

Change Your Moods

"Rejoice in the Lord always; again, I will say, Rejoice."
Philippians 4:4

4. *Cultivate the happiness habit.*

I think it was Abe Lincoln who said, "I've noticed that people are generally about as happy as they make up their minds to be."

I'm proud of the children in our family. They have a very basic, even, positive keel as far as their moods and cycles are concerned. With rare exception, they have a very even-tempered mood of positive attitudes.

I believe this is due to the fact that, to no small measure, when they were younger, we had them memorize the following words of Ella Wheeler Wilcox.

"I'm going to be happy today, though the skies are cloudy and grey. No matter what comes my way, I'm going to be happy today."

Take a few minutes now to memorize these lines and say them each morning when you awaken. It really works.

> **Jesus, help me to cultivate
> the happiness habit.**

Change Your Moods

"As a man thinketh in his heart, so is he."

Proverbs 23:7

5. *Get the happiness habit by turning the thinking dial.*

One of my favorite poets is Santayana, the Spanish philosopher. Of all my favorite lines in prose and poetry, I enjoy his words on faith the most:

> "O World, thou choosest not the better part.
> 'Tis not wisdom to be only wise
> And on the inward vision close the eyes.
> But it is wisdom to believe the heart.
> Columbus found a world and had no chart,
> Save one that faith deciphered in the skies.
> To trust the soul's invincible surmise
> Was all his science had his only art.
> Our knowledge 'tis a torch of smoky pine
> That lights the pathway but one step ahead
> Across a void of mystery and dread.
> Bid then the tender light of faith to shine
> By which alone the mortal heart is led
> Into the thinking of the thought divine."

When the American forces moved into Italy and liberated a small village, they found that old philosopher Santayana in a back room of his house writing a book. When they asked him how he could be creative enough to write a book when the war was all around him, he said, "I have trained my mind to think on eternal matters."

**Think of
divine thoughts!**

Change Your Moods

"It will be healing to your flesh and refreshment to your bones."

Proverbs 3:8

6. *Use your body to change your mind.*

Sound strange? It has been scientifically established by psychiatrists and psychologists and students of the human personality that even as the mind affects the body, the body affects the mind. If you feel low, and if you allow your body to get drooped in a chair, you will feel more depressed. What should you do? The following exercise will help!

   Stand up straight!
     Stretch your body!
       Take a deep breath!
         Throw your shoulders back!
           Lift your chin up!
             Open your eyes wide!
               Flex your muscles and say,

"With the grace of God, I am strong!" Then put your two feet apart, feel your full height, feel your full stature. Before you realize it, your body is changing your mood. God created you this way.

**With the Grace of God,
I am strong.**

Change Your Moods

"Behold, thou desirest truth in the inward being; therefore teach me wisdom in my secret heart."

Psalms 51:6

7. *Reprogram your memory bank.*

Do you know that your moods are determined primarily by a recording of past experiences, an encounter with present experiences, or an expectation of future experiences?

A human life starts with a dot that symbolizes the beginning of the trauma of your birth, the emotional tactile results of the sensation of body touching body, the voice of your mother. That tape recorder is recording every experience through the tactile touch, through the eye, and through the ear; everything is recorded here. It never stops. If your emotional experiences recorded the first few years are basically pleasant, you've got a good tape going. When something painful occurs, however, a nasty bit of static and aggravated assault is on your tape recorder. Every once in a while that anguish or hurt wants to break through. The ugly memory is repressed, but belches forth in the form of an ugly mood. It's still there, and needs to be handled effectively.

Whether it's a guilt lurking in your past, or a hurt, a resentment, jealousy, or an abuse you just can't forget, the answer is the same—Jesus Christ is the way to reprogram your memory bank.

> **Lord, erase my hurtful tapes and
> replace them with Your beauty.**

Change Your Moods

"Whereas, the aim of our charge is love that issues from a pure heart and a good conscience, and sincere faith."

1 Timothy 1:5

8. *Cleanse the roots of your spirit.*

I planted some little palm trees in front of our house and was happy with the results of how they looked. But a few months ago, when the florist came to deliver some flowers, he looked at one palm tree that by now had turned yellow and said, "That palm tree has about had it." "Well, it's got some green fronds on it," I said. "But look at the core of it," he continued. "It's very yellow. In fact, I don't know if you can save it." When I asked him what he thought was wrong he said, "I think the water has sloped off the hill and hasn't gotten down to the roots. The only thing that is going to save it is deep treatment."

He recommended a fertilizer, a long pipe to stick way down in the ground to penetrate all around the roots, and he said, "On the surface you might not see anything, but it will feed the roots. Dig a hole and put the hose all the way down there and very slowly let the water ooze out every day. Tie all the fronds on top in one little bundle and you might save it." I did, and the tree is flourishing.

People attend church week after week and get the sprinkler treatment. And for some, that's enough to keep their spirits green like grass. But others need the deep treatment, the kind of treatment that happens only when you ask the Holy Spirit to come in and fill your life with Jesus himself.

> **Lord, fill me with Your
> life-changing love!**

Change Your Thoughts

"By virtue of that one single offering, he has achieved the eternal perfection of all whom he is sanctifying. The Holy Spirit assures us of this."

Hebrews 10:14, 15

God has a plan for your life and for mine. Are you really filled with happiness, hope, joy, courage and faith? If not, is it possible for your life to totally and completely reverse itself into a positive experience? The answer to that question is very important, and I happen to believe it is yes—human nature can be permanently changed!

I believe every human being has buttons deep within that cause him to be the person he is and react the way he does. Those buttons represent a person's command center or power point.

You can never change human nature unless you touch a person's buttons. Push the red button and POW, change results. Push the green button and WOW, change results. People change when the right button is pushed.

Lord, I give You permission to push the right buttons in me to change me into the person You want me to become

---

**God, help me
push the right button.**

Change Your Thoughts

"Now in putting everything in subjection to Him, he left nothing outside His control."

Hebrews 2:8

The typical approach of psychologists, psychiatrists, and the average clergyman has been to attempt to change people through the rational approach. But my opinion is that people never change from rationality, they only change when you touch their buttons—when they are turned on emotionally.

Another way to express this concept is by saying alter your altars and your whole life will change. What do I mean by an altar? Every person has one. It's the control center deep within you, that source of emotional nourishment that turns you on. Every person has this command center. Touch it and it sparks. Hit it and you hear things. The hidden command center, the control center, the power point, is your altar.

For some people it's their ideology. For others, a personal philosophy of life. And for some, their value system.

Do you know what your altars are? Can you think of a situation where you reacted, or overreacted, because someone pushed one of your emotional buttons?

> **Lord, You're in charge of
> my control center.**

Change Your Thoughts

". . . Jesus stood up and proclaimed, 'If any one thirsts, let him come to me and drink.' "

John 7:37

You can choose the buttons that will be pushed in your emotional control center by controlling your thoughts. Change is possible if you push the right button, but keep in mind that changes for better or worse can occur.

In a letter from Viktor Frankl, the esteemed psychiatrist of Vienna, Austria, he shared the following:

"I notice, having recently returned from America, that everybody there is on a pleasure kick. I declare to you that those who make pleasure their main goal in life are doomed to failure. This is because man is then no longer told by his driving instincts what he must do and he is no longer told by his traditional values what he must do. Those who no longer know what they want to do and have no purpose in life will fall victim to conformity, doing what others do, and pleasure and materialism will not fulfill them. Not ever."

Let's check your altars. Will your altars really bring you happiness, peace of mind, and lasting joy? Or are they the source of your major aggravation, irritation, tension, and trouble? Whatever you do, make sure that your altar doesn't alter you for the worse.

> **My joy comes in being transformed to the person You want me to be.**

Change Your Thoughts

"But lay up for yourselves treasures in heaven, where neither moth nor rust consumes and where thieves do not break in and steal. For where your treasure is, there will your heart be also."

Matthew 6:20, 21

Someone once said the most sensitive nerve in the human body is the one that leads to the pocketbook. In 1923, a very important meeting was held in Chicago, Illinois. Attending the meeting were nine of the world's most successful financiers. It was a high-powered group of people—men who knew the secret of making money. There was no doubt where their altar was.

Let's take a look at where they were 25 years later, in 1948. The president of the largest independent steel company, Charles Schwab, died bankrupt after living on borrowed money for five years previous. The president of the greatest utility company, Samuel Insull, died a fugitive from justice, penniless in a foreign land. The president of the largest gas company, Howard Hopson, was insane. The greatest wheat speculator, Arthur Cuttor, died abroad, insolvent. The president of the New York Stock Exchange, Richard Whitney, had just been released from Sing Sing. A member of the President's cabinet, Albert Fall, was pardoned from prison so he could die at home.

All of these men knew how to make money, but not one of them learned how to live. If money is one of your altars, ask God to make you aware of how you can change.

> **Lord, You are my altar.**
> **Therefore, I have peace.**

Change Your Thoughts

". . . What mighty works are wrought by His hands!"
Mark 6:2

No psychiatrist, no psychologist, no behavioral scientist has had a greater authentic, documentable record of changing people deeply, permanently, or lastingly than have we who minister in the name of Jesus Christ and in the power of God.

Do people really change? Can you alter your altars? Some of you may remember Bill Sands, author of the book *My Shadow Ran Fast.* He was such a tough crook he was listed as incorrigible and not eligible for parole. He was sentenced to solitary confinement in Sing Sing. The warden at the time was a man named Duffy who believed he could transform people through his Christian love. He believed that the worst person could be totally transformed and changed into someone beautiful, and he wanted to try to reshape Bill.

One of the chief executives in the prison had an argument with Warden Duffy. It was turning into a real head-pounding inter-office war. Finally Mr. Duffy's opponent said, "Leopards don't change their spots." And Warden Duffy said, "I don't have any leopards in Sing Sing. I only have people. And people change." Bill Sands did. He was completely, totally, and permanently changed.

> Lord, You can refine and reshape me.
> I'm ready.

Change Your Thoughts

"My sheep hear my voice, and I know them, and they follow me."

John 10:27

In a fascinating report by Dr. H. E. Gruber, he told of the study he did of draft resisters in the United States during the controversial Vietnam conflict. Dr. Gruber felt that most of these men would be of a particular political stripe; a certain emotional type; perhaps reactionary or rebellious; and certainly someone who had had a traumatic psychological encounter which resulted in their rigid draft resistance.

He was wrong on all counts as the following story demonstrates. Dr. Gruber said, "The case I'm about to give you is typical." One young man, who happened to be a politically conservative, emotionally stable, nonreactionary, nonrebellious type, was waiting for a bus. He went into a nearby drugstore and began browsing through the paperback books. He happened to pick up one book in particular and read a couple of pages. A couple of lines grabbed him and caused him to think differently. When he put the book back on the shelf and walked out of the drugstore, he had made a turn around, even though he didn't know it yet. But emotionally and ideologically instead of going one way, he went another and as a direct result eventually became a draft resister. The outcome, the difference in the destination, was tremendous.

In that moment a thought entered his mind at a very deep level, pushed one of his buttons, and he was permanently changed.

**Lord, You lead.
I'll follow.**

Change Your Thoughts

"For what will it profit a man if he gains the whole world and forfeits his life?"

Matthew 16:26

Is God really first in your life? Or is there something more important such as money, power, pleasure, material possessions, or another person? When you put Jesus first above all other things in your life, your life will be changed . . . and so will you! Permanently.

Your thoughts are powerful, so be sure that what goes into your mind will produce a positive thought. Give your mind to God today and let Him provide the thoughts, ideas, and dreams He would like you to have. Together you and God are more than enough to overcome any negative-producing stimuli.

GOD IS FIRST IN MY LIFE.

> Lord, help me to keep
> my thoughts on You.

Change Your Destiny

"I say this prayer to you, Lord, for at daybreak you listen to my voice and at dawn I hold myself in readiness for you, I watch for you."

Psalms 5:3

Possibilitizing means imagining, visualizing, praying, multiplying, overcoming, anticipating, toughening, maneuvering, rebounding, and overpowering the problem! During the next few days, we'll look at these points more closely. For today let's talk about *possibilitizing is imagining.*

When God's presence comes into your life through Jesus Christ, love is going to come into you. This love will so overpower the negative thoughts you will be able to possibilitize your way out of any situation. Possibilitizing is imagining that things are going to get better; they're not going to stay the way they are.

Problems really become serious when they get you to take your eye off your goal. If you imagine things are going to get better, you will be in a frame of mind to contribute to their getting better instead of getting worse.

On a sundial in London, England, is this statement: "It's always morning somewhere in the world."

> **Lord, enlighten my imagination**
> **with Your possibilities.**

Change Your Destiny

"There is hope for your future, says the Lord."
Jeremiah 31:17

Possibilitizing is visualizing victory beyond the battle of the hour. It's seeing the victory instead of the battle. It's seeing the ultimate reward instead of the pain. It's seeing the crown instead of the cross.

Spurgeon, the great Methodist minister, was once talking with a farmer friend out in the country. They saw a cow with its head over a stone wall, looking out into the distance. Spurgeon asked the farmer, "Why would that cow be looking over the wall?" And the farmer answered, "That's simple, because she can't see through it."

In your life you're going to have problems, setbacks, rejections, disappointments, discouragements, and prayers that don't seem to get answered. God may not seem to be around. You may really hit bottom. You'll run into a stone wall. When that happens and you feel you can't cope, do what the cow did. *When you can't see through the wall, look over it!*

Look to the rainbow, the prize, the happy ending, the success, the victory. Look to Jesus. Keep your eyes out into the distance, your goal ahead, and you'll respond with greater confidence in the problem areas.

> **Lord, the vision of victory is before me. Help me to see Your answers instead of my problems.**

Change Your Destiny

"And in the morning, a great while before day, he rose and went out to a lonely place, and there he prayed."

Mark 1:35

Possibilitizing is praying. If God has control over your life, He will not let you quit. You'll be in a possibilitizing mood which is praying: "Father, Your will be done. This, too, will pass; it cannot last."

A listener to Hour of Power sent me this beautiful poem:

"She used to say to me when things went wrong,
Why make them worse with worry and regret?
Lift up your heart and join the merry throng
And in the rush of hope you will forget.

Nothing is lasting in this changing sphere.
The troubles that now seem more than you can bear
Will all have vanished in another year
Like smoke that melts in the morning air.

Time soothes our wounds and stays our falling tears,
And from our shoulders lifts the galling yoke.
No sorrow is as lasting as it seems.
The dark cloud that now obscures the gracious day
Will soon be severed by the sun's white beams
And in the glow of noon will fade away."

Remember to keep on praying! After Good Friday comes Easter morning!

Prayer changes me.

Change Your Destiny

"And I am sure that he who began a good work in you will bring it to completion at the day of Jesus Christ."
Philippians 1:6

Possibilitizing is multiplying the results. Some of you are tempted to quit because you don't see the returns and the results. We've had Sunday School teachers quit because they didn't think they were doing a good job; they couldn't see the results. I know of ministers who have given up the ministry because they thought they were failing. If only they would keep on possibilitizing!

I was inspired by the following story of George Smith, the Moravian missionary. All his life he wanted to be a missionary to Africa, and he finished his preparation and traveled there. After a few months, he was expelled. He left behind only one convert, an old woman. He came back home and soon died. Think of it. All his life he was preparing . . . he went to Africa. . . . spent only a few months . . . came home and died a very young man! But one hundred years later that mission of one old woman had grown into 13,000 happy, black Christians!

Any fool can count the seeds in an apple, but only God can count the apples in a seed. Possibilitizing—multiply what's going to happen.

**Projects dedicated to God
mean multiplied results.**

Change Your Destiny

*"For whatever is born of God overcomes the world; and this is
the victory that overcomes the world, our faith."*

1 John 5:4

Possibilitizing is overcoming rather than allowing yourself
to be overcome.

Pat Shaughnessy, a minister, was at the PanAm air-
counter in August when a bomb went off and killed three
people. He suddenly found himself without his leg, which
had been blasted off near the hip. When I heard he was still
in the hospital, I asked him how he was doing. He laughed
at the other end of the line and said, "It's fantastic how God
doesn't let anything happen to us unless it's great!" He went
on, "You know, losing my leg isn't that bad. I'm sure people
who have never had it happen would say it's impossible to
live without a leg. But it isn't really that bad. I've got my
brain. And I've got my mental attitude straightened out.
And guess what? In two weeks I'm going back into the pulpit again, after an absence of nearly three months. I don't
know if I'll be preaching in my wheelchair or sitting on a
stool, but I'm going to be back, and it's going to be the greatest Sunday in the history of our church."

I asked him, "What's the key? What's the real reason you
can have such a positive attitude?" And he said, "When
you've got Jesus Christ in your heart, everything else is so
exciting that all of the problems you have are really unimportant."

Lord, I trust You to do great things
with whatever happens in my life.

Change Your Destiny

"For God is at work in you, both to will and to work for his good pleasure."

Philippians 2:13

Possibilitizing is anticipating that good will come out of what may look like a bad situation. As President Ford's wife said when she went through her surgery, "I'm confident, secure, and relaxed, because I believe that God will use this to do a lot of good for a lot of people." And there were a lot of women who had an examination and were saved from dying of cancer.

Possibilitizing is toughening yourself. It's keeping up the exercise! Keeping up the training! Keeping up the working. Keeping up the studying. Keeping up the roadwork. Being tough on yourself. Possibility thinking doesn't make success cheap and easy. No success ideas will work if you don't.

Keep on possibilitizing!

**God, help me
to keep on possibilitizing!**

Change Your Destiny

"Hope thou in God."

Psalms 42:5

It's a fascinating thing to study human beings! I have specialized in this for nearly a quarter of a century as a minister, counselor, and author. And I can report to you that under stress, human beings will usually react in one of four ways:

1. Some people will *mope* their way through their troubles. They quickly surrender to self-pity, which gives rise to bitterness.

2. Other people *dope* their way through: They use narcotics from a bottle, a box, or a bag.

3. Lots of people just *grope* their way. They get so confused they don't know where they're going. They lose sight of God's plan for their life by taking their eyes off the goal when they start groping.

4. And there are those who *hope*. In that hope they find the *power to cope*. So they make it.

**Coping power is found
in the hope of Jesus Christ.**

Change Your Destiny

"Henceforth, there is laid up for me the crown of righteous-ness, which the Lord, the righteous judge, will award to me on that Day, and not only to me but also to all who have loved his appearing."

2 Timothy 4:8

I want to share with you the incredible power of hope and what it can do in a human life.

In Calcutta a few years ago, I visited Mother Teresa's "Home of the Dying." When Mother Teresa saw people dying in the streets, she dragged their sick bodies into a deserted temple, which she had cleaned, and there she loved them until they passed away. "Every human being at least deserves to have somebody loving them while they are dying," she said.

The home was overflowing with men in one section and women in another, but it smelled clean and sweet! One of the nurses told me, "It's interesting. We only take people here who are dying. But the amazing thing is when they come here, they feel the love of Christ, they receive hope, and they stop dying. We're going to have to change the name of the place from the 'Home of the Dying' to the 'Home of the Living.'

Where there's hope, there's life! That's the incredible power of hope.

> **Hope gives me
> renewed life!**

Make Your Dreams Materialize

Possibilitize

"Call to me and I will answer you, and will tell you great and hidden things which you have not known."

Jeremiah 33:3

Profoundly and powerfully God has created into every human being the potential for inner peace and spiritual vitality. We need only to know how to tap it and unlock it.

Too often our problem is concretistic thinking. Our thinking is like concrete. If you are in that position, I invite you to change your mental attitude and become more of a plastic thinker. You've probably had a concretistic attitude toward prayer, toward God, toward Jesus Christ, and toward the Holy Spirit. I invite you now to open your mind and dare to believe what you have never dared to believe before: that there is built within you and every other human being, the potential to have a dialogue with God.

What I want to say to you is this: God wants to talk to you. He has not only built into you a relaxation response, He has built into you the receptive capacity to hear His silent voice. Spend the next few moments in quietness listening closely to His voice.

> **Two-way prayer gives me the capacity to hear the voice of God.**

Possibilitize

"Be anxious for nothing, but in everything by prayer and sup-plication with thanksgiving let your requests be made known to God."

Philippians 4:6

1. Possibilitize. Believe that it is possible for God to reach you and speak to you.

2. Sterilize. Cleanse your mind of any sins by accepting Jesus Christ as the Savior of your soul and claiming His promises to forgive you, to cleanse you, and to declare you to be perfect and clean.

3. Neutralize. Put your self-will in gear and say, "God, I'm ready to hear anything You want to say to me."

4. Tranquilize. Relax. Breathe deeply—breathing in faith, peace, and love; and exhaling tension, anger, and resentment.

5. Visualize. Picture a scene of peace, the face of Jesus, or the cross.

6. Harmonize. Prayer is a two-way process. God speaks to you and you speak to Him. Be ready to listen. Ask, and you will receive. God will give you your heart's desire.

7. Actualize. The purpose of meditation is to receive God's message in order to go out and do what He wants you to do—make your life and your world a more beautiful place.

If my prayers don't work, it's probably because there is too much of me in them and not enough of God.

Possibilitize

"If you then, who are imperfect, know how to give good gifts to your children, how much more will your Father who is in heaven give good things to those who ask him!"

Matthew 7:11

Creative prayer is the first step to trustful expectation. When I pray, I expect that God will guide me into what He wants me to do. I trust that the expectation will be fulfilled. After you have practiced creative prayer, God will give you a dream. If the idea comes from God, it will be impossible. God's ideas are usually bigger than our own. Therefore, you have to face impossible dreams with possibility thinking.

Possibility thinking believes that an impossibility can become a possibility, if you affirm it, believe it, declare it, and refuse to give it up. Possibility thinking says that if an idea comes from God, even though it's impossible, be totally for it. Then be willing to move ahead. Wait and see how in the world God is going to solve your problem.

Pray now. Listen to God's answer. Write down the "impossible dream" He gives you.

> **Creative prayer plus possibility thinking
> will never let a problem stop me.**

Possibilitize

"Then you will call upon Me and come and pray to Me and I will listen to you. And you will seek Me and find Me, When you search for Me with all your heart."

Jeremiah 29:12, 13

I like to awaken early while it is still dark and begin my day with this prayer and meditation: "It's possible for God's Holy Spirit to so control my life and thinking today that He can do everything that needs to be done. I will make no mistakes at all because He will control every decision."

Believe that it's possible for you to stay in a two-way dialogue with God. Believe that it's possible to be empowered by God to face pressure with inner calmness. Believe that it's possible to "feel tranquil" in times of tension!

Take these moments to write your own prayerful meditation to begin your day.

_____

_____

_____

_____

I believe it's possible!

Possibilitize

"And the prayer offered in faith will restore the one who is sick, and the Lord will raise him up, and if he has committed sins, they will be forgiven."

James 5:15

Years ago a mother brought her four-year-old son to me. "Dr. Schuller," she said, "you've been preaching about possibility thinking and that all things are possible with God. My son is deaf. I'm sure if you would pray for him he would be healed." I have never felt called by God to go into a specialized healing ministry. But this woman insisted. So I went into two-way prayer. "God, do you want me to touch him and pray for healing?" And the thought came into my mind, "Yes." So I put my hands on this little boy's ears and prayed, "Dear God, help this little boy to hear." I clapped my hands, but he never heard a thing. Two days later, the boy was holding on to the rear bumper of a car and was accidentally dragged behind it. The car threw the little boy and he rolled over and over landing at the curb. His mother picked him up and after a moment he opened his eyes and seemed well. The amazing thing was, he was able to hear! And he has never had a hearing problem since!

> I know God hears
> and answers my prayers.

Sterilize

"Therefore everyone who hears these words of Mine and acts upon them, may be compared to a wise man, who built his house upon the rock."

Matthew 7:24

I spoke to a young lady recently who said she was offered a diamond by a young man. She's been single for many years. I suggested that she make a commitment of her life to Jesus Christ. She asked me, "What does that really mean?" I told her, "Receiving Christ is like receiving a diamond. It means you make a commitment to him and he makes a commitment to you. There is an intimate relationship between the two of you—together you begin to build your future and the rest of your life. You trust him and he trusts you. You share secrets with him that you wouldn't share with anybody else." That's the way it is with Jesus Christ, too.

God offers you a diamond to wear on your heart. And the diamond's name is Jesus Christ. Will you accept God's diamond today?

I accept God's diamond—
Jesus, the rock of ages.

Sterilize

"You were washed, you were sanctified, you were justified, in the name of the Lord Jesus Christ, and in the Spirit of our God."

1 Corinthians 6:11

Cleanse your mind of any sins by accepting Jesus Christ as the Savior of your soul and claiming His promises to forgive you, to cleanse you, and to declare you to be perfect and clean.

Ask Him this question: "Do You want me to become a Christian, Lord?" If the answer is yes, then just say in Your own way, "Jesus Christ, I accept you now. I receive You now. With Your help I'm becoming a Christian right now." Now ask Him this question: "Lord, as I live my life, will You be with me? Will You keep straightening me out, Lord, when I keep making mistakes? Thank You, God. Amen."

I am cleansed. I researched my innermost life, every dark little corner, and I put my uncovered sins at the cross.

Sterilize

"He who has ears, let him hear."

Matthew 13:9

Some people hear a word but it never enters their minds. They're thinking about their own thoughts so they never really hear. What they hear is like seed falling on hard ground. It sprouts a bit, but it doesn't last long. On the other hand there are people who hear with an inner ear in the depths of their subconsciousness with what some psychologists might call integration, without emotional blockage. They really hear and their whole life is changed.

God speaks to you through your inner ear. As you hear Him, life is transformed—you become like a fruitful plant that bears fruit. Two-way prayer is when you speak to God. You ask Him questions and you listen and wait. And, in God's timing, you will hear His voice.

> **I will be still and thrill
> to the voice of the Lord.**

Sterilize

"Behold, I stand at the door and knock: If anyone hears my voice and opens the door, I will come in to him, and will dine with him and he with me."

Revelation 3:20

In your prayers begin to hear a knock at the door. Ask God to come into your life. Ask the Holy Spirit to come into your life. Ask Jesus Christ to come into your life. Ask the Spirit of God to dwell at the depth of your being and answer your questions. Begin with questions like this: "O God, do you have greater lessons to teach me? Do you want me to make some changes in my life? Lord, I have some habits I should break. Father, are there sins in my life that I haven't dealt with? Jesus, am I really a Christian?"

Spend these moments really praying through these questions. As you receive God's answers, remember to thank Him for giving you the power and forgiveness to become what He wants you to be.

My prayer is asking God to make me the person He wants me to be.

Sterilize

"Blessed are the pure in heart, for they shall see God."
Matthew 5:8

What is humility? Humility is to be willing to do what God wants you to do and be what God wants you to be. I suppose that's the reason many people do not succeed in two-way prayer. Their pride stands in the way. The spirit of humility is this attitude: "Lord, speak. I'm listening. Lord, I'm willing to make changes in my life. I'm willing to become a Christian if that's where it starts."

Two-way prayer works miracles if you understand the substance, the strategy, the style, and the spirit. Begin with the spirit of humility by saying, "Jesus Christ, do You want to come into my life?"

Ask God what changes He would like you to make in your life. Listen. Write them down, now.

_____

_____

_____

_____

**Yes, Lord,
I'm willing!**

Sterilize

"Therefore if any man is in Christ, he is a new creature; the old things have passed away; behold, new things have come."
                                        2 Corinthians 5:17

Let's pray. Close your eyes. Go into a meditation in your own way. Relax your body. Remember the soul is trapped in your body. Sometimes God can't get through the tension of the muscles to get to the core of your soul. Be very open and informal with God. Now, ask Him these questions and listen for a thought to come into your mind.

Has my ego been in the way? Jesus, will You come into my life? I feel a peace, Jesus, and it's wonderful. I sense a power and a spirit and it's wonderful. It's very real and I want whatever it is, Lord. Come into my life, Lord Jesus, come in today. Come in to stay. Now listen and you may hear Him say, "I have come in. I have redeemed you. You are mine."

> **I am born again—
> I am clean and fresh and new!**

Sterilize

"Thy kingdom come. Thy will be done, on earth as it is in heaven."

Matthew 6:10

I looked at the front wheels of my car just the other day and noticed that my tires were worn on the sides. I discovered, too late, that my front wheels were out of alignment and so the rubber had worn unevenly. Now I need to get new tires and have my front wheels realigned. Then I'll get maximum mileage.

The reason why many people don't get maximum mileage out of life is because they need to have their "wills aligned." You probably need a will alignment more than you need a wheel alignment. That's what two-way prayer can do. In two-way prayer you line up your will with God, and He lines up His will with you. Only then do you get maximum mileage out of life. As you get power in prayer, miracles happen. God speaks to you and you hear Him. Not with your audible ear, but with the inner ear.

I'm going to realign my will!

Tranquilize

"Be still and know that I am God."

Psalms 46:10

Let's practice two-way prayer: Begin by relaxing. Close your eyes and block out the distractions of the world. Relax. Meditate and focus your mind on something that will tranquilize you. The relaxation response will begin to work. As you relax, don't beg God, don't argue with God, don't demand something from God, but quietly wait until you feel the stillness.

As you go into two-way prayer, allow yourself to wait patiently after each sentence you address to God, giving Him a chance to (a) answer your questions; (b) react to what you have said to Him; (c) communicate a new and relative idea into your mind. He will answer and speak, in the pauses, through the ideas that will come quietly floating into your mind.

**I will wait for God's answers
to my questions.**

Tranquilize

"Peace I leave with you; my peace I give to you."

John 14:27

Jesus Christ is unequaled in producing peace at the deepest level. When you pray, focus on Him. If you want to use a verbal sound, say, "I am." Think of the words, "I am the way, the truth, and the life; no one comes to the Father, but by me." (John 14:6) *I AM* the way into greater consciousness. *I AM* the truth through the awareness of God, *I AM* the life. Follow me and you will have abundant and eternal life. You will feel high and strong. "*I AM* the resurrection and the life; he who lives and believes in me, though he die, yet shall he live." (John 11:25)

When you come out of your "closet of private meditation," you will feel refreshed. You have a new surge of energy. You have new vitality. You have a spiritual high!

God has given me
His peace.

Tranquilize

*"And the peace of God, which surpasses all comprehension,
shall guard your hearts and your minds in Christ Jesus."*
                                                    Philippians 4:7

Meditation is like crossing a stormy sea. You arrive into a
quiet harbor, go into your relaxation, close your eyes, and
shut out the distractions. You breathe quietly, slowly, and
deeply. You probably meditate on a word. Deep tranquility
comes into you. You tap into powerful peace.

However, if you only meditate you haven't gone far
enough. What is needed is something deeper than meditation. If meditation is coming into the harbor, then prayer is
stepping off the ship onto the shore and into the arms of
your Father who has been waiting for you.

Probably the best book on meditation, *How to Meditate,*
by Dr. Lawrence Le Shan, states: "All people who meditate
say the same thing. In meditation they get the feeling that
they are coming home." That's a beautiful feeling. But there
is something more important than coming home—it's what
happens when you get there. In two-way prayer you start
talking to God. He starts talking to you. He gives you guidance in a very clear way.

**I'm going to step into
my Father's arms.**

Tranquilize

"And His name will be called Wonderful, Counselor, Mighty God, Eternal Father, Prince of Peace."

Isaiah 9:6

Visualize Christ coming into your life. Close your eyes and picture in your mind a beautiful scene, perhaps a lake, perhaps a mountain scene. Picture Jesus Christ walking across an open field. You feel that He is a beautiful person and one of your closest friends, but you cannot place Him yet. As He comes closer you can tell by His stride that it is Christ. He is your Savior. He lifts His head and sees you. You see Him. He calls out to you and then breaks into a full run with arms open to you. He is your Lord. You are not embarrassed. You are not ashamed. You open your arms and He embraces you. There is silence. He just holds you. He just loves you.

"What a friend we have in Jesus, all our sins and griefs to bear. What a privilege to carry everything to Him in prayer."

Draw Jesus into your life and you will have peace at the center—enough to face the storms of life!

> **Jesus brings peace
> to the center of my life.**

Tranquilize

"Let us therefore draw near with confidence to the throne of grace, that we may receive mercy and may find grace to help in time of need."

Hebrews 4:16

I'll never forget the day more than 27 years ago when our entire farm was destroyed by a tornado. I remember seeing my dad, an arthritic old man of sixty-six, hobble down the road with his cane. He stepped over the sparking wires, walked across the empty yard, and then came back to us. And we prayed. Through the tears there was a peace and a quietness. Out of the peace and quietness came guidance.

Guidance, peace of mind, tranquility, and power all came through prayer. When I talk about meditation, I'm not talking about some fad that has just been imported from another country and is now sold for a certain amount of dollars. I'm talking about the kind of meditation and prayer that is offered to you free from Jesus Christ! It's been around two thousand years. It works when the roof falls in, when the walls cave in, and when the floor gives way underneath you.

You can achieve the peace and tranquility that produces power through prayer.

**Prayer brings me peace
in the midst of the storm.**

Tranquilize

"Be still before the Lord, and wait patiently for him."
Psalms 37:7

How can you communicate with God to catch His Spirit? How can you catch a dove? Have you ever been to San Juan Capistrano where you can see so many white doves? I used to go there with my little children. They would run after the doves because they were sure they could catch them. They would chase them and almost get their hands on one, only to have the dove slip away. The way to catch a dove is to put your hand out and wait. The dove will come and sit in your hand!

When you start praying, you probably start with, "Dear God," and you keep right on talking until you get to, "Amen." Then you sign off, pull out, and go to work. But you've never given God a chance to speak to you. You never took time to hear. Real communication in all interpersonal relationships isn't a matter of your dominating the conversation and then closing the door and running off. You're never going to build any kind of effective communication unless you spend as much time listening as you do talking.

How do you catch a dove? You get the Spirit by waiting, giving God a chance to talk to you.

I'll catch a dove today!

Tranquilize

"Even though I walk through the valley of the shadow of death, I fear no evil; for thou art with me; thy rod and thy staff, they comfort me."

Psalms 23:4

A dear friend of mine, Louise, was left paralyzed and speechless as a result of a gunshot wound. I called on her a while back in the hospital. "Louise," I said, "there will be many hours when I will not be at this bedside and there will be no members of your family here and there will be no nurses. You will be lying here with the weights pulling on your legs and on your head, unable to move your head to the right or left. And you will be alone. Then what will happen? God will be here! How will you know He's here? In your mind you will hear His words saying, 'I am with you.' Close your eyes now. You can hear His words, 'I am with you.'"

Do you have a bigger problem than Louise right now? Would you exchange problems with her? As of this moment she is still alive. She has found the power to handle her problem, no matter what happens. "I am with you."

**Nothing can separate me
from God's Love.**

Harmonize

"Delight yourself in the Lord; and He will give you the desires of your heart."

Psalms 37:4

Too many people think of prayer as a crisis, panic-stricken dash to God, the all-powerful doctor, to get an immediate solution to their problem. Prayer isn't a matter of getting God to do something for you as much as it is asking God to make you the person He wants you to be.

I ask you to imagine this: You are in a little boat near a sandy shore. You throw out an anchor and pull on the rope until you feel the sandy shore beneath your feet. Then you step out onto the shore. What have you done? You haven't moved the shore to the boat; you've moved the boat to the shore.

> Real prayer isn't trying to get something;
> it's an attempt to become someone. Lord, make
> me the person You want me to be.

Harmonize

"He must increase, but I must decrease."

John 3:30

In two-way prayer God speaks to us more than we speak to Him. That's where the power lies. If most of your prayer-time is spent with you doing the talking, then you can be sure you are in the prayer more than God is. And if some of your prayers don't work, it's probably because there is too much of you in them and not enough of God in them. You have to do less talking and more listening so that there can be less of you and more of God. That's where the power comes from.

Spend these next few moments in prayer. Remember— listen to Him.

Less of me—more of God.

Harmonize

"Let me hear thy loving kindness in the morning; for I trust in Thee; teach me the way in which I should walk, for to Thee I lift up my soul."

Psalms 143:8

One busy morning I realized I was running late. I started praying, "God, I want to spend about fifteen or twenty minutes praying, but I have a problem because I should get out and start running again this morning. I haven't been running for two weeks. But I have an appointment in the office. If I spend fifteen minutes meditating and thirty minutes running, I'll be late. I don't know what to do." All I heard was, "Get out and run." "But, Lord, if I get out and run now I won't spend enough time praying." Again He said, "Get out and run." I said, "But God, you mean you don't want me to spend fifteen minutes meditating and praying?" And He said, "Get out and run, I can talk to you while you're running, too." I said, "Okay, Lord." I jumped out of bed and went out to run. And you wouldn't believe what I accomplished that day in my office!

I can only attribute it to the guidance of the Holy Spirit of the Eternal God. I was in tune with Him and He with me! And out of that meditation I saw greater possibilities, and unbelievable things happened.

> **Possibility-thinking meditation
> will change my life!**

Harmonize

"For the Holy Spirit will teach you in that very hour what you ought to say."

Luke 12:12

Have you ever found yourself in a spot where you didn't know what to say?

I'm a great believer in the Holy Spirit, that power of God Himself who can penetrate the human mind through ideas, moods, flashes, insights, concepts, and inspirations. Two-way prayer is when you go into a quiet place to talk to God. Ask Him questions—that's the key. Don't list all your problems. Don't make a lot of statements. Don't make demands. Don't list all your appeals. Cynical, self-centered, arrogant prayers can kill two-way prayer. Instead go with one thing—questions. Mountain-moving prayer—I hope you can catch it. It works!

My prayers can move mountains!

Harmonize

"Let the words of my mouth and the meditation of my heart be acceptable in thy sight, O Lord, my rock and my redeemer."
Psalms 19:14

W. Clement Stone once said, "The greatest power available to man is the power of prayer." I do not believe there can be ultimate solutions to the poverty program unless you're in tune with God's Spirit. God is the source of all supply. It is God who makes the seed rupture and send its tender shoot through the soil, reaching to the sun. The seed is the source of all life, in seeds and in humans. Get in tune with God's Spirit. That's creative prayer.

Do you have a problem of lack? The first question you have to ask yourself is, is the problem due to a disharmony in my own life as it relates to people, to society, or to God Himself? Get in tune with God's Spirit through creative prayer.

Let's suppose your problem is lack of money. Do you begin by praying, "Dear God, help me to get rich?" Of course not. Begin by praying, "Dear God, where is my blind spot? Where am I failing in my thinking?"

What is your problem today? Spend some time getting in tune with God's Spirit now.

My problem isn't the end of the road—
it is a God-given bend in the road.

Harmonize

*"Then you will call upon Me and come and pray to Me, and I
will listen to you. And you will seek Me and you will find Me
when you search for Me with all your heart."*
                                        Jeremiah 29:12,13

There are four kinds of prayer. The first level is petition;
you draft a request and go to God and say, "God, I want
this." That is the only kind of prayer many people know.
With all due respect, it is probably the lowest level of prayer
because it tends more often than not to be selfish.

The second level of prayer is called intercessory prayer,
which means to intercede in behalf of someone else. You
pray for me and for my needs and I for yours. We pray to
God to help somebody else.

Praise and worship is a third kind of prayer. This is when
people who know and love God pour out their hearts in rev-
erent words saying, "Thank you, God, for what you've done
for me." That is almost the highest level of prayer.

Frank Laubach in his book *Prayer, the Mightiest Force on
Earth* says, "Two-way prayer is the highest form of prayer."
That is when you talk to God and then listen and wait for
His answer. You're not coming to God with any specific de-
mands for yourself or for anybody else and are not even
there necessarily to praise and thank Him. You're there for
guidance. You need to be shaped. You need to be molded.
You need to be made into the person He wants you to be.
That is the purpose of two-way prayer.

> **Prayer is asking God to make me
> the person He wants me to be.**

Harmonize

"I sought the Lord, and He heard me, and delivered me from all my fears."

Psalms 34:4

Prayer is not a solo. Prayer is a duet. To have effective praying, don't come to God and sing a solo. Sing in harmony. Listen to God while He listens to you. Talk with each other until the two of you are harmonizing. Feel harmony in the prayer. Make prayer a two-way communication.

I remember a time when I was going down a mountainside flat on my back in an ambulance with broken bones and bleeding kidneys. I had fallen while in the mountains and was in great pain. I began to practice harmonizing prayer, two-way communication, saying, "Lord, why did I fall, anyway?" And I heard Him say, "Schuller, it's your own miserable fault. You shouldn't have used such a rickety ladder." "That's right, Lord. It's my own fault. Lord, I hope I'm not too badly injured." I heard Him say, "Don't worry. You've got two kidneys and only one is hurting. You'll be okay." And so it went all the way down the hill, over an hour in the ambulance. The attendant said to me, "Don't you want a pain-killer?" And I answered, "No, I'm having too good a time talking!" Prayer is a harmonizing experience!

Prayer is a duet.

Actualize

"Thou art my rock and my fortress; therefore for thy name's sake lead me, and guide me."

Psalms 31:3

Ask God questions. That's the basic style. (In petition you go to God and tell Him you want something. In intercession you tell Him you want Him to do something for someone else. In praise you thank Him.) But in two-way prayer you ask questions. "Lord, am I moving in the right direction?"—and you hear the voice say yes or no. You may think you are talking to yourself, but you're not. That's one of the exciting things that Viktor Frankl says in his book. He says, in effect, unless you are aware of the fact that the conscience is a transcendence that results from your original divine heritage, you will think that you are only talking to yourself. But in fact you are not talking to yourself. It is God speaking to you.

What is He saying to you in your prayers today? Write down the answers and believe they are from Him:

_____

_____

_____

> **I can hear God's voice.**

Actualize

"Draw nigh to God, and He will draw nigh to you."
James 4:8

Two-way prayer performs miracles. It's the ultimate solution to loneliness. I recently read the book *You Are No Longer Alone* by Joan Winmill Brown. Joan was four years old, living outside London, England, when her mother came to her with her suitcase in hand and said, "Joan, I'm leaving for a while. In about a week I'll see you again and I'll have a surprise for you." Joan couldn't wait. The week passed and someone picked Joan up and took her to a house. She came eagerly expecting to see her mother again with a special gift. But instead she entered a room where the shades were drawn. Her mother had died in childbirth. Her life started downhill at the age of four, having lost her mother. In writing this book, Joan told me, "When I began to write my story, it forced me to recall my life. And I remembered that my mother carried a suitcase when she said she'd come back in a week and give me a gift. In recalling that I realized why every time my husband, Bill, left with his suitcase, I shuddered." Her life really came together when she found Jesus Christ and had a beautiful relationship with Him and enjoyed what I call two-way prayer.

> **With two-way prayer—**
> **I am no longer alone.**

Actualize

"Him that comes to me I will not cast out."

John 6:37

"Fear not, for I have redeemed you; I have called you by name, you are mine. When you pass through the waters I will be with you; and through the rivers, they shall not overwhelm you; when you walk through fire you shall not be burned; and the flame shall not consume you. For I am the Lord your God" (Isaiah 43:1–3). My mother said to her pastor, who was there moments before she passed away, that she had heard these words flowing through her mind. It was God speaking to her. "I will be with you, so you will never be alone in life or in death. And never alone in eternity."

Two-way prayer is the ultimate solution to loneliness. Now, of course, you can't try two-way prayer unless God is a friend. And you cannot have communication with somebody you don't trust. If you've had a fight or a spat or if there is an emotional problem between you and another person, you can't communicate. You have to dissolve the negative feelings first. You can only communicate if you're friends. And before you try two-way prayer, be sure you are a friend of God.

> **I am redeemed—God loves me
> and wants to be my friend.**

Actualize

"He shall call upon Me, and I will answer him; I will be with him in trouble; I will deliver him, and honour him."

Psalms 91:15

I was traveling East once when a family told me this story of how two-way prayer helped them to move their mountain. They had three beautiful girls and were looking forward to their fourth child. Their son was born and shortly thereafter the doctor told them that the child was a Down's syndrome (mongoloid) child.

I remember the mother said to me, "Dr. Schuller, we looked at this situation and saw it was an enormous, terrible problem, an awful mountain, an obstacle to the pathway of joy in our lives. Our first reaction was one of anger, then bitterness, then self-pity. It was a vicious cycle of negative emotions. Then we became jealous of other parents who were having normal children. It was terrible.

"Finally, we went into two-way prayer and said, 'Lord, could there be any good in what has happened to us?' And we waited. We heard a thought in our minds and the thought was a very strong, 'Yes.' Then we asked, 'God, what good could possibly come out of this problem?' This sentence came to my mind. 'I will teach you a new dimension of love!' That changed everything! We love our other three children, of course, but knowing that our one child is limited is teaching us a new and deeper dimension of love. What has happened because of that in our mental attitude is a miracle."

> **Two-way prayer can help me
> move my mountain!**

Strive to Come Alive

Strive to Abide

"He who dwells in the shelter of the Most High will abide in the shadow of the Almighty."

Psalms 91:1

As Christians, we believe in success. Why? Because the alternative is disaster. God is not honored in our poverty or sickness. He is glorified in our accomplishments! The Bible holds the key to success.

"Let us lay aside every weight and sin which clings so closely, and let us run with perseverance the race that is set before us, looking to Jesus, the Author and Perfecter of our faith . . ." Hebrews 12:1.

Personally and publicly, this text has been the secret of my success and the success of this ministry. I have summarized the entire teaching of this verse into one single word—STRIVE.

S—Start
T—Try
R—Reach
I—Involve
V—Verify
E—Exert Every Effort, Expending Energy Endlessly

> **I can succeed
> if I will STRIVE.**

Strive to Abide

"Let me dwell in thy tent forever; Let me take refuge in the shelter of thy wings."

Psalms 61:4

Start! Start by looking to Jesus. He is the Author, the Composer, and the Architect of your faith. He is the creative source who writes His bright ideas and beautiful plan on the blackboards of your mind. To strive you have to start. And you have to start right.

I've often told the story of my little boy, Bobby. I remember when he was small and tried to button his shirt by himself for the first time. He began his task enthusiastically, but he started all wrong. He put the first button in the second buttonhole. I tried to help, but he got offended and said, "I can do it." So I watched as he continued to put the second button in the third buttonhole, etc. He got to the top button with no hole to put it in. Carefully correcting him, I said, "Bob, let that teach you a lesson. If you start out right, you'll end up right. But in any project and any effort, be it business, school, relationships, personal fitness programs, whatever, if you don't start out right—it isn't going to end up right."

> **If I start right,
> I will end up right!**

Strive to Abide

"O Lord, who may abide in Thy tent? Who may dwell on Thy holy hill? He who walks with integrity, and works righteousness, and speaks truth in his heart."

Psalms 15:1,2

How do you start out right? A building starts with an architect. A book starts with an author. You must start with a dream. You author an idea with plans to begin. An author is a creative person—the better the author, the greater the dream. Look to Jesus, the Author of our faith. I never start anything until I feel sure that Jesus is telling me to do it. Whether it's to prepare a message, develop a television ministry, build a cathedral, or write a book, I don't dare start unless I really pray about it. Start with Jesus. Let Him be the Author. Let Him write the plan in your mind.

If you look to Him, you also become a possibility thinker. As the Author and Perfecter of your faith, He'll begin by giving you an idea. From that idea, He'll perfect your faith. And as you look to Him, the Bible promises help to "Lay aside the weight which clings so closely." These are weights of negative thinking. Thoughts such as: "I can't do it"; "It won't work"; or "I don't have the connections."

Look to Christ. He is alive. Pray now, asking God to give you a new idea.

> **God is real, and He will give
> you His ideas.**

204

I'll Survive!

"Mercy and truth are met together; righteousness and peace have kissed each other."

Psalms 85:10

I am reminded of the story of the great man Warden Lawes who worked at Sing Sing, the world's most notorious prison. For twenty years he spent his life literally transforming it into a truly humanitarian place.

When Warden Lawes came to Sing Sing in 1921, he brought with him his young wife and three little children. Within the group of vicious murderers and so-called animals, his family made its home. People warned them, "It's dangerous here. These people are murderers." Catherine would reply, "But my husband is here to take care of these men, and I shall love them, too."

So Catherine started reading the records and found out about the different men. She taught the blind to read Braille and the deaf-mute how to communicate. She ministered to the needs of prisoner after prisoner. But then came the tragic night in 1937 when Catherine was killed instantly in a sudden car accident. In a matter of minutes the news was out that the warden's wife had been killed in an accident. They say that the hardest thugs wept as they cried, "Our lady was killed last night." Jesus Christ lived inside Sing Sing Prison through Catherine Lawes.

> **The secret of my success is to find a need and fill it—fill a chasm and bridge it.**

I'll Survive!

"Unto you that fear my name shall the Sun of righteousness arise with healing in His wings."

Malachi 4:2

The time of the singing of the birds has come. When do the birds start singing? In the morning? Yes. In the noontime? Yes. In the setting of the sun? Yes. How do the birds start singing? If you wake up very early you know that the birds do not start singing in chorus. Rather, there is always one solitary note. One bird starts to sing alone until he wakens another bird, a sleeper. And then two birds sing and wake up others. Then there are three, four, and soon a chorus of birds singing. But always it starts with one bird.

That's how it will happen to you. The time of the singing of the birds always starts with one idea that comes into your mind. Let me give you that idea now. This is the single idea, the solitary note, the awakening music that I give you now is one sentence from Jesus Christ: Come unto Me. Come unto Me.

"Yes, Jesus, I will come."

I'll Survive

"The Lord thy God in the midst of thee is mighty; He will save, He will rejoice over thee with joy; He will rest in His love, He will joy over thee with singing."

Zephaniah 3:17

On Christmas Eve, December 24, 1980, our top publicity in two national magazines and over 18,000 persons overflowing the candlelight services at the Crystal Cathedral, I had every reason to be elated. Yet, I went home depressed. I was lower than I had ever been, because I was ashamed of the sermon I delivered. As far as I was concerned, I had failed.

On Christmas Day, I smiled and pretended to be happy, but I had to step out of the house and take a walk in the garden alone. There I had a very meaningful message come into my mind, and I knew it was God. The words were, "I will reward you for what you did for me last night." And I said, "No, Jesus, I don't deserve it. I did an awful job." And He said, "But you were faithful, Bob. You told people about Me, that I am alive." I said, "Yes, I did tell them about You." And He repeated, "For that I will reward you."

When you pursue a dream and have made a commitment, but things get tough and you can't walk away from it, listen carefully. For then of all times a single, solitary warble of a lone bird comes from the branch of a tree. A note of hope comes at the low time of life.

He knows when I need my enthusiasm restored.

I'll Survive!

"He is loving and kind and rewards each of us according to the work we do for Him."

Psalms 62:12

My father was an Iowa farmer, a very devout Christian man. He used to tell me the story of the day the preacher came to call and saw all of the corn growing in straight, clean rows. Then he looked over at the waving acres of glowing wheat and said to the farmer, "Look at the corn, look at the wheat. Isn't it beautiful what God has done with this farm?" Nodding, the farmer said, "Yeah, but you should have seen it when the Lord had it all by Himself!"

God needs you and me to do His work today. In a world where so many people need help, there's no excuse to say, "I don't make a difference." The birds start singing when you're given a challenge, an invitation, and an opportunity to help.

God needs you. Your life does have value.

Make a list of the work God wants you to do for Him today.

_____

_____

_____

_____

My life makes a difference!

I'll Survive!

"Keep up the good work and don't get discouraged, for you will be rewarded."

2 Chronicles 15:7

A group of life insurance salesmen was having a convention in a big downtown hotel. The president spoke and said, "Look, times may be bad, but success goes to the person who ignores the times and sets great goals." He continued, "It is amazing what you can do if you try." Then he gave his men this assignment. "Take a break for ninety minutes, and go across the street to that thirty-five-story tower and each go to separate floors. Go to the front desk of every office and ask the first person you meet the most negative question you can think of."

And with that he dismissed the salesmen. They went through the tower and asked everyone the same question, "Times are bad, aren't they? You don't want to buy life insurance, do you?" Do you know what happened? In spite of such negative attitudes, they all made at least one sale.

If a negative thinker can succeed, what do you think you can do with a positive attitude? No matter how bad the times are, no matter how negative your image of yourself is, you must try. If you try, you will succeed!

**The world is waiting for me
if I try.**

I'll Survive

"And let us not lose heart in doing good, for in due time now we will reap if we do not grow weary."

Galatians 6:9

I was born and raised in a good Holland Dutch community in northwest Iowa. As a child I attended church religiously at the little country chapel called the Dutch Reformed Church. In that conservative Dutch culture, smoking was very proper. In fact it was almost to the glory of God to smoke a cigar, pipe, or cigarette. If you were a good preacher, you smoked. I started smoking when I went to college, and it soon became a regular habit. Before I knew it, I was hooked. I smoked two packs a day for twelve years. Many times after I realized I was addicted, I tried to quit. Finally I came to the conclusion that it was no use, I would never quit. I had tried and tried, over and over again, and I couldn't do it.

Then on January 1, believe it or not, I made a New Year's resolution. With all of the possibility thinking I could muster, and all of the prayer I could manage, I decided once again to permanently quit. I remember praying, "Jesus, with Your help, I'm going to quit smoking and never start again. Liberate me, Lord." And amazingly He did! It's been over fifteen years since I've smoked. I have to say it was Christ working through me. But I had to be willing to try again.

What is that nagging habit you've been trying to lick?

Liberate me, Lord!

I'll Survive!

*"Seeing that we are encompassed by such a great cloud of wit-
nesses, let us lay aside every weight that does so easily beset us,
and let us run with patience the race that is set before us, looking to Jesus the Author and Perfecter of our faith."*

Hebrews 12:1,2

It's not enough to arrive and be successful, for success is
never certain, even as failure is never final.

Why should a person strive for success? Isn't that a pretty
selfish objective? No. For when we succeed, whether it's in
school, marriage, business, or social services—we inspire
others to try to win too. When we fail, we scare a lot of other
people who back away and refuse to try. "Seeing we are encompassed by so great a cloud of witnesses. . . ."

Success is not a selfish objective for there is no way you
can succeed unless you find a need and fill it; find a hurt and
heal it; find a problem and solve it! If you're in business,
people aren't going to come to your store because of your
name and fame. They will only come if you can help them.

How do you succeed? First lay aside every negative
thought, the weights that easily beset you. Put off pessimistic
thinking, thoughts like, "I can't do it!" "I'm dropping out!"
"I'm folding up the business!" Dissolve negative thinking al-
together!

I have a stewardship to attempt to succeed for
the glory of God and for the inspiration of others.

I'll Survive!

*"But they that wait upon the Lord shall renew their strength.
They shall mount up with wings like eagles. They shall run and
not be weary; they shall walk and not faint."*

Isaiah 40:31

I've always had a problem with my weight. As a kid I was
superfat. Today by the grace of Christ, my weight is under
good control. Having never been an athlete growing up in
school, I was always the kid who, when it came to choosing
sides for teams, was never chosen. You can imagine the
wonder I felt when ten years ago a member of this church,
Walt Frederick, came to my office and said, "Bob, you're
going to be a runner." "Me? A runner?" I asked. "Yes," he
said, "The Lord appointed me to be your trainer!" "The
Lord didn't tell me you would be my trainer!" I rebuffed.
"Well," he said, "The Lord's telling you now."

So that began a beautiful exercise routine for me. And
this morning I got up once again to run a few miles. It was
early, the stars were still out, and in the clear sky, I suddenly
heard a rooster crow. The morning was about to dawn. The
birds came out to sing. I returned home just as the dawn was
breaking over the distant hills, and as I showered to prepare
for church I thought, "If anyone had told me fifteen years
ago that at age fifty-four I'd be out running a few miles,
feeling like a million dollars, I'd have said they were crazy."

**I can do more than I think I can if I'll only
strive—start with prayer, then try!**

I'll Thrive!

"Without me you can do nothing."

John 15:5

Striving means involving others in a team effort. When we were in the process of building the Tower of Hope here on the campus of the Crystal Cathedral, we planned to put a 90-foot cross on top of it. But one day the architect, Richard Neutra, called me and said, "Schuller, I know that you have announced that the cross would be 90 feet tall, but it can only be 30 feet tall. If we put up a 90 foot cross, vibrations will run through the tower, crack the concrete and the windows will fall out. It can't be done." As he continued to explain the whole law of aerodynamics to me, I interrupted and said, "Look, Mr. Neutra, this is ridiculous. There is a 300-foot rocket standing on a pad in Cape Canaveral. Why can't you put a 90-foot cross on the tower? Go to the people in NASA and ask them how." And so he did. They agreed that it could be done and explained how. "It will work," they said, "if we avoid vibrations by simply making the base a little wider than the top." And that's what they did. Today the cross stands secure despite occasional earthquakes and heavy winds.

"God can do great things through me if I don't care who gets the credit."

I'll Thrive!

"I can do all things through Christ who strengthens me."
Philippians 4:13

Some say it doesn't make a difference what you believe in as long as you are sincere. The truth is it does. If you're an atheist and believe in nothing, your personality and human value system will be affected. If you're an agnostic and are not willing to make a commitment, your life-style will be affected. You'll never make decisions so long as risk is involved.

I believe in Jesus Christ—He is the Author and Finisher of my faith. I also believe you have talents you haven't tapped yet. You have energies you haven't used. You have abilities you haven't tried.

With Christ as your strength, you can take risks and make decisions. Faith allows you to try before you are assured you will not fail. You have to face a commitment to do something great even though it holds the vast possibility of public disgrace. Only then is there no chance of your success becoming an ego trip. That makes faith! And that takes trust. Trust and respect yourself. God does not give beautiful ideas to dumb people. You can do it. Try!

What are some things you believe in? Write them down.

_____

_____

_____

> **What you believe
> does make a difference.**

I'll Thrive!

"In my troubles I pleaded with God to help me and He did!"
Psalms 120:1

All success starts with an attitude that is positive. Just recently I heard the story of the executive in New York who was heading for the subway late one night. As he walked along, he heard fast footsteps coming up behind him. A little frightened, he looked out of the corner of his eye and saw a mugger following him. He quickened his pace, but the footsteps came closer. When he realized he couldn't outrun his follower, he suddenly did a very smart thing. He slapped his pockets, whirled around, looked the mugger straight in the eye and said, "Hey, you don't have sixty cents on you by any chance? I've got to catch the subway and I'm flat broke!" Caught off guard, the mugger said, "Uh, yeah, I guess I do." And he gave the executive two quarters and a dime!

That's possibility thinking! That's turning an obstacle into an opportunity—a problem into a possibility. A positive attitude can take anything and turn it into an advantage. That's faith! That is what Jesus Christ did with the cross. Show me any other person who lived such a simple life, died such a shameful death, and is so superfamous today. You can't. Nobody comes close to Him.

> **I will turn my obstacles
> into opportunities.**

I'll Thrive!

"Be glad for all God is planning for you. Be patient in troubles, and prayerful always."

Romans 12:12

Thinking positively makes a radical difference in how you live. In reading my diary the other day, I was reminded of an Air Force tour I took years ago at the Kadena Air Force Base in Okinawa. I was met at the airport by Colonel Bill King of Selma, Alabama. He shared with me the story of his childhood and what a victim of real prejudice he was. "I was just a poor little black boy," he said, "and every day I used to watch the trains go through town. Every time the caboose faded from sight and I heard the last wail of the train's horn, I used to think, 'Will I ever get out of Selma?' That is how bad we were treated. But I became a Christian. That made a difference. I never became angry when I was mistreated. I just moved ahead and built a good life for myself anyway. Had I reacted negatively to my situation, I would have missed seeing the good that was still there."

That's what you call attitude!

No matter how negative my situation is —as soon as I react negatively, I'll miss the good that is still there!

I'll Thrive!

"And we know that all that happens to us is working for our good if we love God and are fitting into his plans."

Romans 8:28

The world's largest bell is in Moscow. It stands over 18 feet high and weighs 219 tons. Compared to the Liberty Bell's 2,018 pounds it is the largest and heaviest bell in the world. But the pitiful thing is that the incredible toll of the bell has never been heard. The czar who had it built never heard it ring. During the making of the bell, as the hot metal was being cast in mold, a fire broke out in the factory. In extinguishing the fire, a small trickle of water entered the mold and created a crack. When the mold came off, the metal was cracked and the bell was forever ruined. One trickle of water was all it took to silence the powerful voice that was meant to sing!

What a trickle of water did to a 219-ton bell, so in the same way, a trickle of negative thinking can crack your spirit. One negative thought of self-pity, jealousy, depression, or discouragement can silence the melody of your life. Look to Jesus—the Maker and Molder of your faith. He will give you a positive attitude.

I won't let a trickle of water take the sound out of my melody.

I'll Thrive!

"As one whom his mother comforteth, so will I comfort you."
Isaiah 66:13

I recently had a woman tell me this story about her son:
"Dr. Schuller, I always had problems with my son. He was
totally rebellious and refused to listen to me. I tried both
punishing and consoling him, but nothing worked. One
weekend he ran away and by Sunday morning he had not
returned. I was mad and terribly upset, feeling I was a failure as a mother. It was in that awful mood that I turned on
your program, the Hour of Power. You were making a statement about faith. You said, 'When a problem is beyond
your ability to handle it, then it becomes God's responsibility. Faith is recognizing God's responsibility to handle what
we can't handle.'

"So," she said, "I made this simple prayer, 'O God, my
son is your responsibility. Put him in a place where you can
save him.'" She continued, "You know what? God answered my prayer. God put him in a place where every
Sunday morning he watches the Hour of Power. A few
months ago he wrote a letter, saying, 'Mom, I've been
watching Dr. Schuller and I've given my life to Jesus
Christ!'" She said, "Dr. Schuller," and the tears streamed
from her eyes, "My son is in the Federal Prison at Fort Lea-
venworth. Hour of Power is the only program the prisoners
listen to every Sunday. God put him in a place where He
could save him."

> **With faith I will recognize God's responsibility
> to handle what I can't handle.**

I'll Arrive!

"No one having put his hand to the plow and looking back is fit for the kingdom of God."

Luke 9:62

I had an experience recently that really shocked me. Before leaving on a trip to Palm Desert, my car broke down. A good friend of mine, who happens to be a Cadillac dealer, insisted that I drive one of the brand new Cadillac Seville demonstrator cars. Was that fun! I started the engine, put the car in reverse, and could not believe what I saw. As I backed out of the driveway, suddenly the digital started flashing, and registering the miles an hour in reverse. For the first time in the history of the car industry in the United States, on the brand new Cadillac Seville, there is a speedometer that registers the backward speed!

In times of defeat, it's easy to think of going backward. If we're going backward, let's not count it! The secret of success is to look ahead. We must lay aside the negative weights and run with patience.

**I will look ahead
and run with patience.**

I'll Arrive!

"For I am confident of this very thing, that He who began a good work in you will perfect it until the day of Christ Jesus."
Philippians 1:6

Your project is on its way. You've involved a lot of people who have made a commitment along with you. Now it is time to verify and double-check your basic purpose. Ask yourself, "Am I still on the right track?" It's easy to get side-tracked and forget why you started in the first place.

A lot of churches have grown into establishments, and small businesses into major corporations, and yet have lost their original focus. Get back to the basics. This has been the theme of our church management this year.

The head of one of the greatest banks in America was at a conference with me not long ago. "I'm asking three questions at our executive level," he said. "They are: 'What do we really want to accomplish? If we keep going at it the way we are, are we going to get there? And if we make it, will it really make us feel good?'"

Ask yourself these same questions today. Then rely on Jesus, He'll keep you on the right track.

Am I still on the right track?

I'll Arrive!

"He also that is slothful in his work is brother to him that is a great waster."

Proverbs 18:9

I made a mission trip to Asia during the Vietnam conflict and visited the Medical Air Evacuation Center for the U.S. Army. During the briefing, a general said to me, "Dr. Schuller, so far in the course of this war only eleven people have died in transit. Previously many of our injured died either on a stretcher, in an ambulance, or on the airplane. However, this battle we decided no injured person would be moved unless we were sure he could make it to the next point.

"So," he said, "We have put up a sign all over the medical unit that has three words: CHECK—DOUBLE-CHECK—RECHECK!! Before any man is put on a helicopter, he is checked: Can he make it to the hospital? After he is on the helicopter, we double-check—has his blood pressure dropped? Can he still make it? Finally, as the helicopter is about to take off, he is rechecked. Has anything been over-looked?"

Verification—it will help you too! Check, double-check, recheck! It's the key to success. And verification will avoid waste.

Our biggest problems are not caused by shortage—they are caused by waste. We waste the dream God has for us, or we waste the resources He provided for us. Whether it's physical, mental, or spiritual resources, the key to success is to cut down on waste. My number-one reason for low pro-ductivity can be summed up in one word—WASTE!

**I'll check, double-check, and recheck!
And eliminate waste.**

I'll Arrive!

*"And the Lord said, 'Who then is the faithful and wise stew-
ard, whom his master will set over his household to give them
their portion of food at the proper time? Blessed is that servant
whom his master when he comes will find so doing."*

Luke 12:42,43

I have an unpublished letter, written twenty years ago by
Ronald Reagan. When it was written, no one knew he
would someday become President. But even then, this letter
revealed some of his character that got him where he is
today. The letter is addressed to a man on our church staff,
Michael Nason. The letter itself is unimportant. What does
say something about the man Ronald Reagan is the stationery. A fundamental element of his character is exposed in
the letterhead and return address of the envelope. For on the
address is the name Ronald Regan—misspelled. Scrawled
above the last name in ink is a little "a" to correct the spell-
ing mistake. Do you realize what that says about Ronald
Reagan? Most people would have thrown such stationery
away. He didn't. It wasn't that important. He didn't waste
it—he corrected it. Mr. President, keep it up!

STRIVE! Make sure you are not wasting resources.

Think of some ways you could conserve your resources.
Write them down.

_____

_____

My greatest waste is the
waste of a God-given dream.

I'll Arrive!

"And he dreamed that there was a ladder set up on the earth, and the top of it reached to heaven; and behold, the angels of God were ascending and descending on it!"

Genesis 28:12

The other day I read a story about a little boy looking at a picture. The picture was a huge composition showing the White House in Washington, D.C., and below it a little log cabin. Between the two was a photograph of Abraham Lincoln. A ladder spanned the distance between the log cabin and the White House. When the little boy asked his mother what the picture meant, she explained, "Abraham Lincoln was born in a log cabin, and he climbed the ladder to the White House." The little boy was impressed. But his mother said, "Do you see the words written beneath the picture? It says, 'The ladder is still there!'"

There is a ladder for you too! That ladder is to climb, achieve, and succeed. Success is a matter of one single word—FAITH! Nothing makes a greater difference in life than faith. Everybody has it—even the atheist! The atheist has faith that there is no God. The agnostic has faith in being noncommittal. I have faith. I have faith in God and my faith is rooted in Jesus Christ.

> **The ladder is still there—**
> **I will climb today!**

I'll Arrive!

"Have this attitude in yourselves which was also in Christ Jesus!"

Philippians 2:5

It was the job of a certain lady who worked for the telephone company to give the correct time when people called in for it. Every day at five minutes to noon a man called to ask for time. And every day without fail, she gave him the information. This happened every day, five days a week, every month for twenty-five years. Her curiosity had increased during all those years as to who the man was who called every day so punctually at five minutes before noon. Finally on her last day at work, she decided to ask him. "Oh," the man said, "I'm the man who blows the whistle at the town factory. It has to be blown at exactly twelve noon because everybody sets their clocks and watches by my whistle." "Oh my gosh!" she exclaimed. "For twenty-five years I've been setting my watch by your whistle!"

There must be a "Greenwich mean" in life. There must be a North Star. I'm like a watch—I often get off the track. But Jesus Christ is my North Star. He is my moral and spiritual Greenwich mean time. He gives me direction. Yes—sometimes He leads me through some very deep waters, but then He helps me not to quit.

Jesus Christ is my North Star.

I'll Arrive!

"The Lord will work out his plans for my life—for your lov-ing-kindness, Lord, continues forever."

Psalms 138:8

If God has a plan for your life, there's no reason to be pessimistic. You can expectantly follow His plan and know you will be blessed. God wants you to run successfully, striving to succeed so that you can be a part of a problem. Only successful people can help the people who are hurting. So you and I must succeed! And to succeed, we must "Strive."

Start . . . try . . . and REACH! To reach simply means to try to do the impossible. The greatest personal successes always come when we establish a goal and strive to do more than we thought possible. You must reach farther than you have ever reached before. Do you remember buying your first house, wondering how you would make your payments? How about when you started your own business? You thought you could never get it off the ground. But you did. When you went back to school and went on to get an advanced degree, at the time it seemed impossible. Yet nothing ever happens until you reach beyond your grasp. Tennyson said it: "A man's reach must exceed his grasp, or what's a heaven for."

> **Unless I reach beyond my grasp,**
> **I'm not moving in the arena of faith.**

I'll Come Alive!

"Show me the path where I should go, O Lord; point out the right road for me to walk."

Psalms 25:4

Jesus will give you an idea and God will reveal His plan for you, but it will be humanly impossible. When you ask for guidance, be ready to do what you have to do—try! It's amazing what you can do if you will only start with prayer and try. I'm positive that every human being has exciting possibilities ahead of him that haven't been tackled yet. If you think you can't do what you believe God wants you to do, don't believe it. You can!!

Right now God wants to give you a new goal. He is motivating you to start, to try, and to reach. Let Him write a new idea on your mind, as an author begins a new chapter. Let God's plan shape your life, as you prepare to run with patience the race that is set before you.

Pray right now that God will give you a new goal. Write it down.

Commit yourself to it.

_____

_____

_____

T-R-Y stands for:
Trust and Respect Yourself. I WILL TRY!

I'll Come Alive!

"The Lord your God in the midst of you is mighty; He will save, He will rejoice over you with joy; He will rest in His love, He will joy over thee with singing."

Zephaniah 3:17

Dr. Norman Vincent Peale said it so well, "Most people fail not because they lack talent, training, or opportunity. Most people fail because they don't give life all they've got!"

Some of you are tempted to hold back a little. You're not giving your God-inspired dream all you've got. Strive! Striving begins with starting. Starting begins with realizing you can't do it alone. No man is an island. And success without Christ is impossible. If by accident you did succeed without Jesus Christ, you wouldn't enjoy it. For success is not a matter of how much money you make, the car you drive, the business you build. Success is being the person God wants you to be. It is doing the job He wants you to do; carrying the cross He wants you to carry. And in achieving success, you'll inspire a lot of people to strive, too. Then you'll come to the end of your life with pride behind you, love around you, and hope before you.

This is the beautiful plan God has for you. It's loaded with possibilities. And it all started with Jesus. If you have never done so before, look to Him today. He lived. He died. And HE IS ALIVE AGAIN TODAY TO HELP YOU WIN THE RACE!

> **SUCCESS is being the person
> God wants me to be.**

I'll Come Alive!

"And the time of the singing of the birds has come."
Song of Solomon 2:12

There is not a more beautiful time of the day than when the birds sing. When is that time? The time of the singing of the birds is in the morning when the darkness of the night is gone and the dawn is about to break forth in regal splendor, its golden arm stretching across the sky to bathe the earth in joy and hope.

The time of the singing of the birds is the time when you are given another chance. It's when a new opportunity is born with the beginning of the day. Every day is a chance to start life over once more. God gives us new dreams and new goals. A brilliant idea will come into your mind and just as the concept is conceived, so is the time of the singing of the birds.

Listen!
I can hear the birds sing.

I'll Come Alive!

"And the angel that talked with me came again, and waked me, as a man is wakened out of his sleep."

Zechariah 4:1

There are three kinds of people in this world:

1. There are the doers. They are the ones who make things happen.
2. There are the viewers. They watch things that are happening.
3. There are the sleepers. They don't even know anything is happening.

What kind of person are you? Do you make things happen? Do you watch things happen? Or do you not even know anything is happening?

A friend of mine in the real estate business said that once in a while he finds a product to list, either a house or piece of property, that he calls a sleeper. This piece of property is loaded with possibilities, the price is low, but nobody wants it. Nobody notices that it is a real bargain. It is sleeping, waiting for somebody to discover it. There are a lot of people just like that. They are sleepers, loaded with possibilities, waiting to be discovered. Are you a sleeper? Today you can wake up and step into the circle of life and discover the dream God has for you.

> If I'm a sleeper, it's probably because I think
> I don't have what it takes. The truth is: I do!

I'll Come Alive!

"For God so loved the world that He gave His only Son, that whoever believes in Him should not perish but have eternal life."

John 3:16

People often ask me, "Schuller, aren't you concerned about poverty? Aren't you concerned about war? Aren't you concerned about oppressed human beings who live under various forms of dictatorship in our world?" My answer is—"Yes, I'm concerned. For at the deepest level, all of these problems have the same root—the devaluation of the human being!"

The deepest need you have is the need for self-worth, self-respect, and self-esteem. You deserve to be treated beautifully, simply because you are a human being. Every human being deserves to be treated like a prince or princess—first class! When Colonel Bill King took me to the airport after taking me on a tour, I said, "Thank you, Colonel. You really gave me a first-class treatment." I'll never forget his answer. He said, "Yes, sir. I did give you first-class treatment, but not because you're white, not because you're Dr. Robert Schuller, and not because you're traveling at a brigadier general rank. I treated you first class for only one reason—because you're a human being. There's only one way to treat any human being—FIRST CLASS!"

How could you treat the people you come in contact with today in a more loving and accepting way?

There's only one way I can treat any human being—FIRST CLASS.

I'll Come Alive!

"So it is that we are saved by faith in Christ and not by the good things we do."

Romans 3:28

It's thrilling to stand where great people have stood! This week I had this experience at the Annual Prayer Breakfast at West Point Military Academy. As I looked out over the 4,200 highly disciplined men and women, I was thrilled! For I was standing where Eisenhower stood. That night I slept in the Thayer Hotel where MacArthur and, more recently, the hostages slept. It's thrilling to stand where George Washington stood and delivered his farewell address. It's always thrilling to be in the footsteps of great people!

However, to stand where the greatest people have stood is not on a platform. Nor is the greatest thrill to sleep in their beds. The greatest thrill is to stand in a position where the greatest people have stood. And that is a position of FAITH!

The bottom line of my life is FAITH.

I'll Come Alive!

"You believed that God would do what he said; that is why he has given you the wonderful blessing."

Luke 1:45

When I married my wife thirty-one years ago, I had faith. That was no argument—it was an act of starting out before knowing how it would end up. When you accept Jesus Christ—you choose to believe. It's actually getting off the fence and quitting the sophisticated role of the cool, coy agnostic. It's an act of belief to commit yourself before you know the final results. That's faith!

Who needs faith? You do! Maybe today, maybe tomorrow—but definitely someday.

How do you get faith? There's no way to get it except by meeting Jesus Christ. No matter who you are, what your religion is, or lack of it, it's a fact—Jesus Christ lived. He believed in God—nobody denies that. He was a fantastic person—everybody admits to that. He didn't have any hang-ups—He was one beautiful human being. When you meet that type of person—you can believe in Him.

I believe in God because I believe in Jesus Christ. If you're a doubter, then I'd rather accept Christ's opinion than yours. When you accept Him, you can become a believer, too.

> **Faith is a choice. I make the decision to be a believer. Who needs faith? I do!**

Problems Are
Masked Possibilities

Fruitful Frustrations

"Fret not yourself because of the wicked.... Trust in the Lord, and do good."

Psalms 37:1-3

How can you handle frustrations that arise as you pursue your goals? Frustration is something everyone experiences.

In the Book of Romans, St. Paul says, "Whensoever I take my journey into Spain, I will come to you" (Romans 15:24). He went to Rome and was thrown into a prison cell and never got out. So he never did go to Spain. St. Paul knew what frustrations were. I am sure you know what they are, too. But how do you handle them?

I want to offer you five simple words that rhyme over the next few days. If you keep them in your mind, I believe they will help you through the months to come.

Frustration is a setup for God to either shape you, mold you, mature you, or guide you along the way. Frustrations can be fruitful if we learn to handle them in a positive way.

What frustrations face you today?

_____

_____

_____

I'll meet each frustration with positive expectation.

Fruitful Frustrations

"If I say, 'I will forget my complaint, I will put off my sad countenance, and be of good cheer.' "

Job 9:27

Don't *tape* your frustrations. Many people record them, remember them, and rehearse them. They tell everybody they meet how frustrated they are. Weeks later they still remember their frustrations.

Dr. Adler, the great psychiatrist who succeeded Freud, liked to tell this favorite joke. There was a group of people all crowded together, sleeping on the floor of a great auditorium during the war. When they were about to get to sleep, one woman would always cry out. "Oh, God, I'm so thirsty!" People would tell her, "Be quiet!" Just when they were almost asleep again, she would cry out, "Oh, God, I'm so thirsty!" Finally one man said, "Can't somebody get her a glass of water?" Rather a simple idea. In the darkness you could hear the shuffle of feet, and then the sound of the woman gurgling the water. But suddenly they heard her again saying, "Oh, God, how thirsty I was!"

Now there is a profound psychological lesson in this little joke. Don't tape it. Don't hold onto it. Many people would feel emotionally lost and lonely if they didn't have past hurts and past frustrations as their morbid friends to keep them company. Don't *tape* frustrations.

**I'm forgetting my frustrations and
proceeding with poise!**

Fruitful Frustrations

"You blind guides, straining out a gnat and swallowing a camel!"

Matthew 23:24

Don't *scrape* your frustrations. They are like mosquito bites. Now I must say in California we don't have many mosquitos, but I was born in Iowa and there we had them.

Let me share with you a fundamental lesson on how to handle mosquito bites. Don't scratch them. There is a distinctive, intuitive itching temptation to scratch them. But when you do, you make them worse, and they won't be gone in twenty-four hours. They'll last a week or more.

Frustrations are mosquito bites. Don't scratch them. You only make them worse.

One of my favorite stories illustrates this point. There was a very frustrated woman on a bus who spouted off and made a scene. She was rude, crude, and abusive. As she was getting off at one of the bus stops, the driver said, "Madame, you left something behind." She walked back up the stairs of the bus and said with a scowl on her face, "What was that? What did I leave behind?" And the bus driver said, "A very bad impression!"

Don't *scrape* your frustrations.

**I'll make my mountain a molehill
with God's help!**

Fruitful Frustrations

"God is our refuge and strength, a very present help in trouble."

Psalms 46:1

Don't yield immediately to the *escape* temptation. Many people want to leave the whole scene. In the years I've been counseling, there have been many wives and husbands who have said, "I wish I hadn't divorced my spouse. My second one was worse."

Someone once asked Socrates, "Should a man get married?" And he replied, "By all means. Every man should have a wife. If you marry a good wife, you will be thankful. And if you marry a bad wife, you can become a philosopher." That's being creative, isn't it?

In periods of great frustration, you may have the feeling that your problems will go on and on, but they won't. Every problem has a life span. No frustration will enjoy eternal life. Every mountain has a top.

What frustration have you been avoiding?

Don't escape your frustrations! Hang on! You'll survive!

> **Lord, help me face my frustration
> and find fulfillment!**

Fruitful Frustrations

"Rejoice with those who rejoice, weep with those who weep."
Romans 12:15

Don't *drape* your frustrations. If you've got a feeling, it's got to come out. You can bury a stone. You can bury a stick. You can bury an old tin can. But you can't bury a worm. The principle is: *You can't bury and repress negative emotions; they will eventually come to the surface.* Then you are liable to blow your stack at the best people in the worst possible times.

Don't try to hide and pretend there is nothing wrong. Develop the ability to open up before you blow up. Try to get to the ones who are the source of frustration in a small, quiet meeting, not in public. Then open up. Try to be as kind as you can, and if you are unkind, apologize.

Be constructive in ridding yourself of your frustrations, and you will find yourself having more energy and enjoyment in your life.

How can you constructively rid yourself of the frustration you listed yesterday? List three ways:

_____

_____

_____

**Joy is handling my
frustrations creatively!**

Fruitful Frustrations

"Those whom [the Lord] loves, he reproves and chastens."
Hebrews 12:6

One of my responsibilities as pastor of my church is to be the general manager of the entire operation—under Jesus Christ. From a human standpoint this means management. So, inevitably and not infrequently, this means frustrations with people on how to handle problems. I made a decision a long time ago, I would never fire anyone even though I have the power to do so. I said, "Lord, you do the hiring and firing. If I have a frustration, I will assume that it means I have to learn something from this. I either have to grow or be taught humility or patience. You take it away if it has to be."

I like the story of the man who had a 100-year-old grandfather clock with a huge weight at the bottom. He watched that old clock having to push that weight back and forth and thought, "That's a terrible burden for such an old clock. It moves so slowly." So he opened the glass case and lifted the huge weight off to relieve the old antique. But the clock said, "Why do you take my weight off?" And the old man replied, "Well, I know it was a burden to you." But the clock exclaimed, "Oh no! My weight is what keeps me going."

Because God really loves you, you will experience frustrations. God has to frequently frustrate us either to teach us patience, to control us, to teach us humility, or to restrain us. Your weights are what keep you going!

**Lord, don't remove my burdens,
just use them to mold me!**

Fruitful Frustrations

"Thou has granted me life and steadfast love, and thy care has preserved my spirit."

Job 10:12

Dr. Frankl explains life with this illustration: A person is like an actor on a stage. You are born, and you are on stage until the end. The spotlight is bright, and it is on you. The houselights are dark. You come onto the stage, and you do not see the audience. There is only a black hole. They have no lines to speak. You do not hear them or see them. But you are very much aware of a presence judging you. It is also encouraging you and probably inspiring you and that knowledge energizes you and motivates you and guides you because it determines your behavior while you are on the stage. If you keep your mind on pleasing the unseen in the black hole, before you know it, the end comes. Then the applause. The lights go on and you finally see the faces. So it is with you and me. God is there, in effect, like a black hole. You cannot see His face. You cannot hear His voice, but you know there is a presence watching you who cares about your performance and is silently judging you. Thus it restrains you, inspires you, motivates you, and encourages you.

Look into that black hole and you will see Christ out in that audience loving and encouraging you. He'll give you the power to turn your frustrations into fruitful experiences.

> **Lord, Your caring love**
> **encourages me to try harder!**

Welcome Interruptions

"I have fought the good fight, I have finished the race, I have kept the faith."

2 Timothy 4:7

How do you handle life's unwelcome interruptions? There are three points I want to share with you on this topic. First, *prevent* many of them. Second, *resent* none of them. And third, *invent* possibilities in all of them.

Let's discuss how to prevent them. For instance, sickness is an unwelcome interruption. Usually sickness occurs when we violate the natural laws. We don't eat right. We don't exercise right. We don't sleep right. We drink or smoke too much. No doubt a lot of people get sick simply because they don't take care of themselves.

I take great pride in the fact that with God's help, I am a runner. But some people pushing fifty are fat and flabby. They have never developed physical fitness in their whole lives. They are prime candidates for heart attacks.

I run every day now. And it's a great feeling to be in top physical shape, to feel your heart going thomp, thomp, thomp. But I pay the price. No less than twenty minutes every morning I am on the road running hard. Everything worthwhile has a high price tag. Many ailments could be prevented with a physical fitness program.

Physical fitness firms my faith!

Welcome Interruptions

"And above all these put on love, which binds everything to-gether in perfect harmony."

Colossians 3:14

In the past quarter century, I have counseled many married couples. I have seen a lot of marriages fall apart, and the unwelcome interruption of divorce comes because the husband or the wife has neglected the marriage. They refused to pay the price of a close relationship.

A lot of unwelcome interruptions can be prevented with a little forethought. All relationships have to be cultivated, seeded, watered, and nurtured in order to grow. So each requires time, effort, and planning.

Unwelcome interruptions can be prevented if we will pay the price, in love and dedication.

To what relationship can you add some preventative love and dedication?

_____

_____

_____

True love dispells frustrations!

Welcome Interruptions

"Great is the Lord, and greatly to be praised, and his greatness is unsearchable."

Psalms 145:3

When unwelcome interruptions strike, never resent them. What you need is the assurance that good will result from the interruption.

A couple I knew had been married for many years and were looking forward to their retirement. They were going to travel and enthusiastically made all their plans. A month after he retired, the husband suddenly died. Life seemed to stop for the wife, too. She put a tombstone on her husband's grave inscribed with the words, "The light of my life has gone out." Many of you who have lost a spouse know what she meant. But with the passing of time and the counsel of her pastor, she came alive again. Two years later, she married another man and began a new life.

"Pastor," she said, "I'm going to have to change that line on the tombstone now." "Why don't you just add one," the pastor suggested. "I struck another match!"

**Lord, lead me to the light
in all life's interruptions.**

Welcome Interruptions

". . . That your faith might not rest in the wisdom of men but in the power of God."

1 Corinthians 2:5

I sat next to a man at a banquet once who told me the following amazing story.

"I pride myself on getting to work on time. If the telephone rings when I am ready to leave the house, I tell my wife to say that I've already left. She usually does, except for one morning. The phone rang and she said, 'Oh, he's just about to leave.' I swore at her under my breath as I went to pick up the phone. Of all people it was the one guy I was trying to avoid. Now he had me cornered on the line. I couldn't cut him off because there were political involvements, and I would've been cutting my own throat. I had to try to keep him happy. I looked at my watch and thought, *If it weren't for this guy I'd be on my way to work.* I would have been on the bridge already, crossing over the freeway at the interchange, halfway there. At that point, my house shook and the ground seemed like water. It was a big earthquake. I read in the newspaper later that the bridge over which I was to have been at that moment had collapsed."

Don't resent those unwelcome interruptions. God may be doing something beautiful through them. Prevent them when you can, but don't resent them when they come.

**God's grace transcends
my man-made goals!**

Welcome Interruptions

"I will instruct you and teach you the way you should go; I will counsel you with my eye upon you."

Psalms 32:8

Invent positive solutions to unwelcome interruptions.

One of the great men of America was the legendary Will Rogers. His great ambition in life was to be a circus cowboy. He finally got an opportunity to perform in New York, but his whole career hinged on one trick—a lariat trick. He was so excited about being in New York with a big audience where he could finally gain fame with his rope trick. But he was so nervous he lost control of it at a peak point and became tangled up in his own lariat. Everybody laughed. Instead of panicking he commented, "Well, getting tangled up in a rope ain't so bad, unless it's 'round your neck!" Everybody laughed again. Then he made another comment, and they laughed some more. He discovered a new talent within himself—the ability to make people laugh. At that moment, he found his destiny.

Lead me, Lord, from the lariat's loop that binds, to your laughter that liberates my life.

Welcome Interruptions

"My soul, wait thou only upon God, for my expectation is from Him."

Psalms 62:5

Invent possibilities. That thought reminds me of when I attended the premiere of Corrie ten Boom's movie, *The Hiding Place.* I had never seen so many celebrities gathered at one time in one place before in my life. It was very exciting. Mrs. Schuller and I were at the door entering the theatre when suddenly a tear-gas bomb went off and everyone went weeping out of the building.

In the street a stage was set up, and Pat Boone was entertaining the people. He called me up on the stage and said to me, "Dr. Schuller, what do you say in a situation like this?" "Well," I said, "this situation is pregnant with possibilities. I have no doubt many times things happen we can't control, but we can control how we will react to them. I'm pleased, Pat, with what is happening here. People are singing hymns in the street."

I would say that most of the thousand people in that crowd were very busy people and made every minute count. But they suddenly found themselves with an hour of time on their hands, which could have been viewed as an unwelcome interruption. Yet so many of them were shaking hands, meeting each other and exchanging ideas. What could have been a frenzied, harrowing experience turned into a glorious victory for Jesus. The minds of these people were centered on Him, and therefore a positive result was imminent.

Lord, let me see interruptions as
beautiful blessings in disguise.

Welcome Interruptions

"Ah Lord God! It is you who has made the heavens and the earth by your great power and by your outstretched arm! Nothing is too hard for you!"

                                                    Jeremiah 32:17

One of my favorite stories is of the beautiful artist Sir Edwin Landseer, a famous artist of animals. One of his greatest paintings is in Scotland. It is on the wall of a beautiful inn that overlooks the rugged terrain.

Some years back during a celebration when the inn was new, somebody popped open a bottle of soda and it sprayed on the newly painted wall before the paint and plaster were dry. Only dirty brown stains running down to the floor were left. The host who owned the place was understandably angry. He evicted the guest, and the party broke up early.

One of the guests was Sir Edwin. After everyone had left, including the host, he locked the door, opened his bag, took out his paint and brushes and the big brown stain turned into a brown rock. Then he painted cypress, evergreens, spruce, and the remaining mountainside. And on the rock, standing on two feet, the Mountain Stag, a goat with his horns curled, a proud beast. Curling around the rock was a mountain stream with white foam.

He turned an ugly stain into a beautiful painting. He invented a positive solution to one of life's unwelcome interruptions.

**Beauty beckons within welcome interruptions.
Lord, let me always see it.**

Creative Competition

"Let us run with perseverance the race that is set before us, looking to Jesus the pioneer and perfecter of our faith."
Hebrews 12:1,2

The key to happiness and peace of mind can be found in today's Scripture. You will come to understand yourself, your highs and your lows, your drives and your drags, your ambitions and your laziness. The key to understanding what makes you the kind of person you are is within this sentence because it introduces us to the words, ". . . run with perseverance the race that is set before us. . ."—the race of competitiveness in human existence.

How do you handle competition? Around that question revolves almost all the important facts and fantasies of life. Life is basically a force that pushes and propels us into competitive situations. For instance, when a new child enters this world, he competes against the very forces of death and an anguished, painful cry is uttered as he calls out for security and food.

Child psychologists tell us very clearly that in the first twelve months a child has to learn trust, because a human organism feels that the new environment itself is a threat to his existence. And a threatening experience is nothing more than a negative reaction to a competitive situation.

**Lord, help me creatively
climb competition mountain!**

Creative Competition

"Speaking the truth in love, we are to grow up in every way into him who is the head, into Christ."

Ephesians 4:15

When two little toddlers get together with one toy, they compete for the toy. When the child is in the twenty-four-to-sixty-month period of life, competition becomes a major factor in determining how he will be the rest of his life.

It has been established that by the time a child is five years old, he or she appropriately identifies with either the mother or the father. A little boy competes against a "big" boy, and a little girl competes against a "big" girl. The competition is a knowing, nonverbalized experience to a child at that age.

A little girl may be sitting at the dinner table jabbering to her mother, when suddenly father who has been working all day and is eager to tell mother something, finally says to the child, "Will you please be quiet and let me talk?" He does not realize he is giving the child an infantile experience of competition.

Competition, then, can be viewed as a threatening experience; and at that tender young age, a child can develop a whole life attitude of how to react to competition. He or she may turn out to be a person who never really wants to succeed because success means competition—and competition is viewed in the mind as a threatening, hostile experience.

How do you view competition? Think about your reaction as you face competitive situations today.

> **Love leads to a healthy competitive spirit.**

Creative Competition

"Do not be comformed to this world but be transformed by the renewal of your mind."

Romans 12:2

A child in school realizes it is a matter of competition for grades, which includes attention to and from the teacher. Unfortunately, too many children equate attention with affection. And if the child doesn't receive adequate affectionate feeding in the home, he probably will do some ridiculous things in school just to win in the competition for attention.

Competition in the childhood level is what makes adolescence so difficult. For the young person is coming to realize he should stand on his own feet and be a mature adult. Yet he finds so much security in the group experience which he finds less threatening because he's just a conformist to the group and not competing. We need to develop the strength to become the person that God intends for us to be, which sometimes means we cannot conform to a group's standards.

Life ultimately can be viewed around this whole theme of competition. Have you had a negative experience with competition? What were your feelings? How did you react? Now is the time to heal from hurts you have experienced because of internally mishandled competition. Take those hurts to Jesus today.

> **Lord, heal my hurts of the past.**
> **Transform my life by living in me.**

Creative Competition

"But thanks be to God, who in Christ always leads us in triumph, and through us spreads the fragrance of the knowledge of him everywhere."

2 Corinthians 2:14

Competition isn't limited to children. Here's one woman's story.

"I happen to be a very smart and successful businesswoman. My husband's business wasn't doing too well, and I began to help him. When I moved into the office, we started making more money than we thought we could. After a while I noticed that my husband began to resent me. I didn't realize until he threatened to pack up and leave just how angry he was. I asked him, 'What have I done? I've tried to be a help to you.' He said, 'You're trying to tell me how to run my business.' I apologized and stopped going into the office.

The business began going downhill. His pride wouldn't allow him to say anything, but I asked if I could help. He wanted me to come in one day a week, and as things improved I gradually began working every day. Business was great. Suddenly without further warning my husband left me. I was devastated. During this period I met Jesus Christ and had a wonderful experience with Him. I called my husband one evening and asked him to come home. He's back now and I have changed. Something of the competitive instinct in me has been altered, and I sense and believe it is for the better. Even though I don't know the ending of the story, I do know I have a peace I've never known before in my life."

> **Lord, make competition a wonderful experience.**

Creative Competition

"But thanks be to God, who gives us the victory through our Lord, Jesus Christ."

1 Corinthians 15:57

Whole psychological systems revolve on the watershed of the issue of competition. Some would say that goals are terrible because they produce and contribute to competition which in turn produces a threat of failure and subsequent neuroticism.

Viktor Frankl, by contrast, believes that goals are very important. They add meaning to life. Tension can be creative. It can be an uplifting force.

Even economic systems in the world today hinge upon how to handle competition. Some hold competition is bad because it puts some people down and therefore we should equalize all of our economy. Everybody should have the same amount, then everybody would be treated fairly and there would be no competition, no wars, no peace, and no tension.

By contrast, the kind of economic system which we have in the United States encourages competition. If viewed creatively and positively, competition can be an enormous challenge, not a threat. It can bring greatness from mediocre people. It can uplift and produce drive, energy, ambition, and enthusiasm.

When Jesus Christ has control of competition, the person who rises to the top does not put the others down, but reaches to lift them up and *everybody benefits.*

> **Lord, uplift me, energize me with the challenge of competition.**

Creative Competition

"Behold, we call those happy who were steadfast."

James 5:11

I counseled with a man some time ago. He had enormous drive. He was doing great. He became an executive vice president in a top American enterprise. Suddenly he lost his drive and ambition. He couldn't understand it until under analysis it came out.

There was another young executive recently hired. He looked upon that other man as a threat because in his opinion that young guy had something up on him. He was afraid that he would never become the chief executive. When that decision was to be made eight years down the line, the young man would have been nine years with the company. They would have seen him as a better man and he would pass him up. In his own mind he reacted to that imaginary competition by mentally retiring.

I said to him, "You have really copped out. You're so afraid of failure that you back away from competition. What would happen? The young man may become chief executive and then you could pat yourself on the back and say, 'Oh, I rose to become executive vice president, but at least I never had a failure in my life.' Not true. You failed when you backed away from healthy competition. You failed when you saw competition as a threat instead of a positive potential motivating force."

What competition is threatening to you today?

Now look at the other side of the coin. Isn't this really a potential motivating force in your life?

> **Steadfast stick-to-it-iveness brings joy
> far greater than I ever imagined.**

Creative Competition

"For by a single sacrifice, he has perfected for all time those who are sanctified."

Hebrews 10:14

The healthiest competition is with yourself.

God has a unique plan for your life and if you've been competing against others, you've been wasting time. Begin competing against yourself.

Be kinder than you ever were.

Be more understanding than ever before.

Give more than you ever gave.

Achieve more than you ever have.

Compete against what you did last year. Do you know what will happen? If every year you just compete against the person you were the previous year, you will find yourself climbing in every way into a more beautiful person. And you cannot possibly lose when you compete against yourself.

Finish this sentence:

Today I will strive to _____
_____ better
than ever before.

Lord, You are the potter, I am the clay. Make me more beautiful today than I was yesterday.

The Greatest Possibility Thinker

"And Jesus increased in wisdom and in stature, and in favor with God and man."

Luke 2:52

Jesus Christ makes all the difference in the world! He is the greatest possibility thinker who ever lived. The truth is He had every reason to grow up to be an impossibility thinker.

An impossibility thinker is someone with a terribly negative self-image who is not only emotionally deprived, but filled with frustration and saturated with hostility. He is intuitively tuned-in to trouble, certain that nothing will work, and definitely his own worst enemy. By definition, this should have been Jesus Christ. By all odds, He should have been a classical negative thinker.

This week we'll be examining the life of Jesus closely. The facts will show that many elements in His childhood and adult life could have contributed to His becoming a negative person. Why didn't He? What can we learn from His example? Over the next few days, let's consider His life and look at Him afresh and maybe see for the first time the Person He really is.

Lord, help me learn possibility thinking
from Your example.

The Greatest Possibility Thinker

"I made known to them thy name, and I will make it known, that the love with which thou hast loved me may be in them, and I in them."

John 17:26

First of all, Jesus was a member of a despised minority. He was a Jew—a victim of racial prejudice. He lived in Nazareth, the crossroads of the world's wickedness. Every thug, hood, and international con-man moved through that town. Taverns were filled with drunken men conspiring to take advantage of people. Being a Jew was bad enough, but to be born in Nazareth was to be alienated from the high class, snobbish Jews from Jerusalem. One simple insulting statement said it all—"He's a Nazarene."

He lived in a society where life was without security. On the average, people died before they were forty years old. There was no penicillin, medicine, or even a dream of a hospital. They were poverty-stricken and abused. Jesus never saw the Forum or Colosseum in Rome, or the glistening white marble Parthenon of Athens. He never got to Alexandria or to Rhodes. He never got to Pompeii or Ephesus. He was untraveled and possibly uneducated. We know He could read, for He went to the synagogue to read from the Scriptures, but apart from that we know nothing of His education.

His environment was a negative one. How did Jesus cope? Compare the society you live in today to see if there are similarities with those in Jesus' time.

> Lord, living in your love exchanges negative experiences for powerful possibilities.

The Greatest Possibility Thinker

"I will tell of thy name to my brethren, in the midst of the congregation I will praise thee."

Psalms 22:22

Jesus belonged to a family with no prestige or high-ladder connections. They were on the low social rung. His father was a simple carpenter. His mother, a peasant woman. Some said His mother conceived miraculously. Others disbelieved and said in fact He was conceived out of wedlock. The rumors He heard, the people He met, the language He was exposed to were the gossip and crudity of the Nazarenes.

He never married. He never had the emotional nourishment and strength that can be drawn from a spouse. He never had the comfort of a close, intimate friend—one whom He could embrace and hold close. He never knew the pride that comes from fathering a son or daughter, especially in a society where a man's real wealth was his children. He lived and died childless with no one *except you and me* to carry on His name.

Christ has no hands but our hands to do
    His work today!
He has no feet but our feet to lead men
    in His way,
He has no tongue but our tongues to tell
    men how He died,
He has no help but our help to bring
    them to His side.

Annie Johnson Flint

Use me Lord, to help others see
possibilities in their problems.

257

The Greatest Possibility Thinker

" 'Lord, how often shall my brother sin against me, and I for-
give him? As many as seven times?' Jesus said to him, 'I do not
say to you seven times, but seventy times seven.' "

Matthew 18:21,22

Carefully study Jesus' life. Psychoanalyze His acceptance
into society—the way people put Him down, misinterpreted
Him, and criticized Him. He was a sure candidate to grow
up emotionally deprived, prone to violence, soaked with
frustration, and destined to be a reactionary—a revolu-
tionary who would lead the guerrillas out of the desert to attack the Romans at night. He'd be a radical terrorist with a
cause of liberation that would build an army of men to
march through the streets and assault Pilate's camp in Jerusalem. Jesus could have easily turned out to be a terrorist.

Jesus, the Man, who had all of the negative stimuli within
His psyche that could have turned Him into a negative radical reactionary, went through His thirty-three years anything but that type of man.

Most of us would have to admit that we have not been
subjected to as much negative stimuli as Jesus. Then compared to His life, ours hasn't been all that bad. We need to
get off the "me" and onto the "He." He is our example. He is
The Way.

> **Forgiveness frees me to live positively,**
> **enthusiastically, even in the midst of a storm.**

The Greatest Possibility Thinker

"Pray constantly."

1 Thessalonians 5:17

Jesus lived in a Jewish colony where some believed He was indeed the promised Messiah. Every Jew awaited the day God would come to the world, born of a virgin, to live like a human, despised and rejected of men just like the prophet Isaiah had written. To many, Jesus was the Messiah. To others, He was a liar.

"My Father and I are one," He said, claiming unity with God the Father. "That's blasphemy!" unbelievers cried.

"I am the Way, the Truth, and the Life. No one comes to the Father but by me." Cynics cried out all the more. Whispers were all over town.

Sure, He preached to thousands who believed He healed many people through His miracles. Yet when He claimed, "I am the Resurrection and the Life. He who believes in me shall never die," even they could not deny the rumors that He claimed to be the Messiah. Jesus had the courage of His convictions. He knew the truth and did not sway from it.

Jesus drew His courage and strength from God, the Father. And He did it through prayer.

Positive Prayer Produces powerful possibilities.

The Greatest Possibility Thinker

"You call me Teacher and Lord; and you are right, for so I am. . . . For I have given you an example, that you also should do as I have done to you."

John 13:13,15

Jesus was accused and put on trial before Pilate, of a crime that was punishable by execution. What had He done except make claims about himself? "I am the Good Shepherd," He was reported as saying. "I know my sheep and no one will pluck them out of my hands."

The Jewish leaders were split in their beliefs. Some thought he was the Messiah. To those who disbelieved they said, "If He is not, what will the Messiah be like?" They looked at His noble life and knew the beautiful person He was. How could a person with such a negative childhood, society, and background grow up with such a positive self-image?

On trial He was asked to clear up the confusion. Pilate spoke, "Jesus, there are people here who claim you are God in human flesh. Tell these poor superstitious peasants they have misunderstood you. Tell the truth—or be convicted for blasphemy, punishable by death!"

When you see how a person responds under extreme pressure and unbelievable stress then you find out the truth in his character. When I see how Jesus responded at His trial— quiet, calm, poised under pressure, there's only one thing I can say for Him. Jesus had class! He was what He claimed to be, and He took His sentence to the end and died for the truth.

**Lord, strengthen my self-image
to withstand stress.**

The Greatest Possibility Thinker

"And I, when I am lifted up from the earth, will draw all men to myself."

John 12:32

Jesus was put to the test even in His final moments. He was the one who said, "If you have faith as a grain of mustard seed, you can say to your mountain, 'Move,' and nothing is impossible." So Jesus, nailed to the tree, was to test His own words. Someone yelled at Him, "Practice what you preach. Come down from the cross. You saved others, save yourself."

But Jesus did not come down off the cross. That would have been the easy way out. An impossibility thinker always runs from his problems. But a possibility thinker welcomes the cross and turns the cross into a crown!

Each person bears many crosses during a lifetime. What is your heaviest cross today? Do you need help to carry that cross? Let your spirit soar to the very throne room of God himself and He will comfort you. But even more than that, He will ask you to leave your burden with Him.

> **Let me see the crown in every cross.**
> **Let me face every problem with enthusiasm.**

The Greatest Possibility Thinker

"In Him, we have redemption through His blood, the forgiveness of our trespasses, according to the riches of His grace which He lavished upon us."

Ephesians 1:7,8

Was it when a blind man grabbed His ankle, felt His hairy leg, and held on to it saying, "Are you Jesus? Can you heal me?" Or was it when He met the harlot and turned her into a lady? Or was it when He preached His dramatic sermon to the audience of 5,000, the Sermon on the Mount, and said, "Blessed are the meek, for they shall inherit the earth. Blessed are the pure in heart, for they shall see God. Blessed are the peacemakers, for they shall be called the sons of God?"

His finest hour was when He turned the cross into a grand possibility. He saw it as a chance to tell the world that there is no sin God cannot forgive. He used it to save a soul even today. To the dying thief He said, "Today you will be with me in paradise." He used it to make a statement that the world would never forget, "Father, forgive them, for they know not what they do." That's class! That's character!

> **Lord, Your lavish gift of forgiveness
> uplifts me and gives me peace.**

The Greatest Possibility Thinker

"I led them with cords of compassion, with bands of love."
Hosea 11:4

Jesus showed us we are not victims of our circumstances!
He showed us how we can handle our stress. "Father, into your hands I commit my spirit," He prayed. He gasped, and He died. The crowd that gathered for the spectacle went home, all but a few followers. The Roman soldier who was in charge of crucifixion recognized Him for who He was, took off his helmet, and became the first Roman to join this new Jewish sect. "Truly, this man was the Son of God," he said as they took Jesus' body from the cross and put it in a borrowed tomb, sealed with a stone. The cross was taken down, leaving only an empty hole in the ground and ashes in the city dump as it burned, charring the last remains of the famous death.

What enormous love for us He displayed when He died. It is difficult to grasp in all its fullness the gift He gave to each of us by that death and then by His resurrection. We have new lives in Him. He loves us that much. Let His love surround you now as you spend a few minutes thinking about His victory.

> **Love lifts me and gives me victory
> in all circumstances.**

The Greatest Possibility Thinker

"In him was life, and the life was the light of men."
John 1:4

The rumors that Jesus had risen reached the remaining disciples—eleven scared, unstable men with whom Christ had spent time. The crook, the politician, the fisherman, and the converted harlot—all came together on Easter Morning now more confused than before.

Thomas said, "No, I cannot believe my Lord is alive. I'll believe it when I see it. Only when I can put my hand on his side and stick my fingers in his wounds will I believe." "Then do so," Christ said as He appeared to them all. "My Lord and my God!" Thomas gasped at the sight of his risen Lord.

Two thousand years later, one billion people in this world believe without seeing. For Jesus rose again and is very much alive today. Through His spirit He lives through me and all who believe in Him. If you don't believe He's alive now—you're the one who is really dead.

Jesus Christ is the ultimate possibility thinker, and today He's telling you that your dreams can rise from the dead, too. Your hopes can rise from the ashes. You can be saved. For God does give life after death.

Follow Him, live with Him—and anything is possible.

Thank you Lord, I'm Alive!
I see Your light that will lead me forever.

Put God's Power
To Work Today

Relieving Power

"So, my dear brothers, since the future victory is sure, be strong and steady, always abounding in the Lord's work, for you know that nothing you do for the Lord is ever wasted as it would be if there were no resurrection."

1 Corinthians 15:58

A student once said to me, "Reverend, I always thought only winners succeed. I never knew losers could succeed, too."

If you have failed in your marriage, your interpersonal relationships, your academic pursuits, in maintaining your own physical or spiritual health, you still can be a winner. If you feel in some way you are or have been a loser, then this message is for you: Losers can be winners, too!

Life is filled with stories of upsets when all the computer predictions and expert projections are thrown to the wind. Your life can be an inspiring upset story, too!

I believe losers can become winners. If you are trailing at the end of the race, you can pull out of the outside. And when you hit the wire, you can be at the head of the pack. First prizes don't always go to the brightest and strongest man. Again and again the man who wins is the man who is sure that he can.

I can be a winner too!

Relieving Power

"She shall bring forth a son, and shall call his name Jesus: for he shall save his people from their sins."

Matthew 1:21

Christ gives us *relieving power*. What does that mean? It means, He relieves us from original sin. You may have heard it said that the church teaches that people are conceived and born in sin. Original sin means that we are born with a negative spirituality. It means we don't have the inherent trust that we should have. To be conceived and born in sin is to be born with a negative self-image. Adam committed a sin. When he did, he became guilty. When he became guilty, he hid in the bushes, having lost his "trusting nature." Immediately he was infected with a negative self-image. The result you have is what is normally called a sinner, somebody who is really rebelling against God.

Yes, we are "born in the bushes." We are insecure and detached from God. So we naturally become "sinners," and suffer from guilt. It is this inherent and acquired guilt that contributes enormously to the will to fail.

Yet, Christ gives us relieving power: the power to relieve us from our sin, our negative spirituality, and our will to fail. What a relief!

**Christ relieves me of my guilt.
What a relief!**

Relieving Power

"For by grace you have been saved through faith; and this is not of your own doing, it is the gift of God."

Ephesians 2:8

Many people want to fail. By failing they think they can expiate for their own sins and guilt. It is incredible what a human person will try to do to earn his own salvation. Some people try to give a lot of money to the poor. Some try to buy their salvation. But you can't buy salvation. It is the gift of God. Don't go out and deliberately fail in order to try to earn your own respect! It won't work that way! You can only be relieved of deep guilt through the cross of Jesus Christ. Only He can forgive.

Salvation is God's gift to me.

Relieving Power

"Neither is there salvation in any other: for there is none other name under heaven given among men, whereby we must be saved."

Acts 4:12

I remember attending a psychiatric congress in a foreign country some time ago. One psychiatrist said, "The basic problem in human nature is insecurity and guilt." And I nodded my head and thought, "Right on!" Then he said, "That's why we psychiatrists are the only people who can heal people's spiritual problems. Because we are uncommitted to moral issues, we are not offended by what people say or do. They can come and tell us all the garbage and all the dirty polluted things they have done. It doesn't bother us. And that's why we can hear and we can forgive."

At that point I raised a question. "Sir, you have made a mistake. If you are not committed to a moral value, then you have not been offended—then you cannot forgive because only the offended can forgive." And there was silence. Because it was true. God has been offended and only God can forgive! (And He wants to!) Trust Him! He wants to come to say that He loves you and wants to forgive you. When you are delivered of guilt, you are relieved of your basic distrust which is the core of your negative self-image

> **Only the offended can forgive.**
> **I know I am forgiven by my God.**

Believing Power

"I can do all things through Christ who strengthens me."
Philippians 4:13

Relieving power produces *believing power.* Relieved of
your basic distrust you can begin to believe that you are a
worthy person. You deserve to succeed!

There are other people who are such losers that the only
way they know how to win is to keep on losing. Now that
may sound strange, but listen carefully: The only way they
know how to win is to lose. By losing they say to people, "I
told you I couldn't do it." It gives them a moment of "winning" in their "failing." When you have relieving power,
you can have believing power. You begin to believe YOU
can do it. What happens when you think you can do it? You
begin to run into people who believe in you! People aren't
going to believe in you if you keep telling them you can't do
it. Insecure people attract insecure people. The first thing
that happens is that you're attracted to positive-thinking
people. They affirm you! They love you! They see the potential in you and they begin to love you because of it!

My love is wanting to uncover the potential
in the people around me today.

Believing Power

"Your faith should not stand in the wisdom of men, but in the power of God."

1 Corinthians 2:5

Dr. Viktor Frankl gave this definition of love: "Love is wanting to uncover the potential in people."

That's how God loves you! It's how Jesus loves you! He wants to uncover the possibilities within you.

Relieving power produces believing power. Believing power is the beginning of success! Because the person you see in your mind is the person you will be!

Michelangelo had a huge chunk of marble that had been cast aside by sculptor after sculptor because it was too long and too narrow. When asked what it was for, he said, "I see David." He chiseled and carved, and when he finished there was David. He saw David in the marble and he created David in the marble.

Pray right now that God will begin to reveal the wonderful potentials He has hidden in you.

> **My believing power is
> my beginning of success.**

Believing Power

"With men this is impossible, but with God all things are possible."

Matthew 19:26

In setting your goals assume that it is possible, even though it may appear impossible.

Adela Rogers St. John has written a marvelous book entitled *Some Are Born Great*. In it she tells the story of Rachel Carson, who wrote *Silent Spring*. In the book there is a dialogue between Alice and the Red Queen. Alice says, "One can't believe impossible things." The Queen says, "I dare say, you haven't had much practice. When I was your age, I always did it for half an hour a day. Why, sometimes I believed in as many as six impossible things before I had breakfast." "And that," says Rachel Carson, "is a very necessary thing to do and to know. If you start believing in impossible things before breakfast, the first thing you know— by dinner time they are not impossible anymore."

> **With God, my impossibilities
> become possible.**

Believing Power

"Whatsoever is born of God overcometh the world; and this is the victory that overcometh the world, even our faith."

1 John 5:4

Let the size of your God set the size of your dream. In other words, make your goals big enough for God to fit in.

Remember, you can never do anything by yourself. If you are a success, it will only be because others made you successful! It is your responsibility to set your goals—God will use others to make them come to pass! That means you begin by drawing support first of all from God Himself. I don't believe that any person will be a happy success without God.

Have you chosen to take God into your life? Have you chosen to accept Jesus Christ into your life as your Savior? You need Him. And so do I.

> **I will make my goals big enough
> for God to fit in.**

Believing Power

"Trust in the Lord forever: for in the Lord Jehovah is ever-lasting strength."

Isaiah 26:4

I want to ask you one question: Are you happy with the goals you've set for yourself? If not, set new ones! Don't tell me you're too old. Don't tell me you don't have the money. Don't tell me you don't have the connections, the brain power, or the will power. That's locked-in thinking. Assuming that there is a solution to every problem, what goals would you set for yourself today?

Let me ask you this: How is your relationship with God? You don't want to set any goals unless your heart is right with God. He says to you, "I have set before you life or death, blessing or curse. Oh, that you would choose life."

Pray about your goals right now. Write down your three most important ones.

1. _____
2. _____
3. _____

**My goals will become my targets
but never my ceilings.**

Believing Power

"And Jesus answering saith unto them, 'Have faith in God.' "
Mark 11:22

Belief. Without a winning attitude, you can't possibly believe in any visionary dream. I shared the technique of positive affirmation and belief one morning on television. I suggested that anyone faced with personal trial or difficulty do as I had been taught. Go to the window and look out at the clouds and the sky and the trees and the birds. That's what I did often as a child. And as I looked at the beauty of the scene God created, I said to myself, "I believe." Those words helped me. They gave me a winning attitude.

When I shared that story, a hardened, old, agnostic colonel in a military hospital tuned into the program at just that point. He listened to what I said and thought to himself, "What a lot of holy baloney." But doctors had told him he was terminal and he was in need of hope. So when the program was finished, he slid out of bed and went through the little ritual. Then the next day, figuring he had nothing to lose, he repeated the process. Those few moments of positive affirmation and belief each day led him to believe first the Bible and then Jesus Christ. He experienced a miracle of healing and became a glorious Christian worker for years before he died.

I believe!

Believing Power

"He shall pray unto God, and He will be favorable unto him; and he shall see His face with joy: for He will render unto man His righteousness."

Job 33:26

God is waiting to answer your prayer, if you will only ask Him to make you into the great person that He wants you to become.

Ethel Waters said it: "God don't sponsor no flops."

I truly believe that the Bible makes one thing perfectly clear, and that is, every human being is God's beautiful plan. When a life gets messed up, it isn't God's fault. It's ours. We don't follow the plan, we don't look for the plan, or we don't give it all we've got.

In the Psalms we read that God made every man just a little lower than the angels. And God has crowned man with glory and honor.

Are you really ready to follow God's plan for your life? Are you seriously intent to have Him as your sponsor? If so, make the commitment today. Let today be the first day of the rest of your life following God's way.

> **God don't sponsor no flops.**

Transforming Power

"Do not be conformed to this world but be transformed by the renewal of your mind."

Romans 12:2

"Do not be conformed to this world but be transformed by the renewal of your mind." What does this mean? If you have tried and failed and tried and failed and tried and failed, chances are you are trying within your own strength and power alone, and that's what is called "conforming to the world."

"The world" is a biblical word that, in the Bible, basically means the total aggregate collection of corporate human beings who are unrelated to God and who are, therefore, basically skeptical, negative-thinking, cynical people. They are the mass of people who have no dynamic, healthy, vital relationship with God. They become cynical people. They distrust themselves, they distrust others, and they distrust God.

There is hope for you! You can be healed, even if you have suffered emotional damage, or you haven't learned self-confidence or decision making.

The Bible says, do not be conformed to "worldly" thinking. This is the kind of mentality that says, "I can't do it. I guess I was born this way. I'll always have this character defect. There is nothing that can be done about it."

"Do not be conformed to this world but be transformed by the renewal of your mind." Now that's the key to succeeding where you have always failed before.

My life can be transformed!

Transforming Power

"The Lord is my strength and song, and he is become my salvation: He is my God."

Exodus 15:2

Dr. Norman Vincent Peale says in one of his marvelous books, "Almost always people fail not because they lack the possibility of inner strength, but because they just don't give it all they've got. They hold back a little bit." You can succeed when you've always been failing if you'll just get that inner strength. Stop flying; settle down. Begin by avoiding these flights. Make the commitment.

How do you stand with God? How do you stand with Jesus Christ? What's holding you back? Maybe it's the fact that just when you are ready to make the ultimate decision that could solve your problem once and for all, you back off. I know that ultimately you will never be the person you want to be. You will never solve the problems that you have until you make a real deep commitment to God and Jesus Christ. And that's how your total life can be renewed and your mind and your life transformed.

I will make the commitment.

Transforming Power

"And let us not be weary in well doing; for in due season we shall reap, if we faint not."

Galatians 6:9

The mental attitude you have will determine the goals you set. And the goals you set more than anything else will determine where you will end up in life, whether it's a spiritual goal, a personal goal, a professional goal or your family goal. It makes no difference.

Sigmund Freud said that goals are very dangerous, because if you set goals and then don't make them, you'll experience failure. Dr. Viktor Frankl from Vienna, Austria, says that goals are great. Indeed, it can be quite disastrous if you set a goal and don't make it and have a negative attitude toward it, but not reaching your goal isn't as dangerous as not having a goal. He likes to point to the Old Testament story of how God always kept a pillar of fire in front of the people at night and a cloud by day to pull the people forward. That's what goals do to us. You never catch up with the cloud. You never catch up with the fire. And the "is," must never catch up with the "ought." If you set a goal and then reach it and can't expand it, you start dying.

What goal do you have before you today?

_____

_____

> **If my goals are not expandable
> they will be expendable.**

Transforming Power

"Commit your way to the Lord and He will crown your efforts with success."

Proverbs 16:3

There is nothing more important to the human psyche than the internal assurance of success. The mother feels this need to succeed as she looks upon her newborn child. The student feels it as he listens attentively in the classroom. The teacher feels the need to succeed as he tries to impart knowledge to young minds. And the businessman feels the overwhelming urge to succeed as he conducts his daily transactions. Those who are Christians know there is nothing more frustrating than the feeling that they are failing in their prayer lives.

Success is a noble word. And I want to share with you how you can be a success. What is the principle of success? I am going to sum it up in one sentence: Choose the winning attitude.

> **I can choose the winning attitude.**

Transforming Power

"We can choose the sounds we want to listen to; we can choose the taste we want in food, and we should choose to follow what is right."

Job 34:3,4

I want to use a word that you may have mixed feelings about. That word is *predestined*. There are some events and circumstances over which you have no control. You did not choose the color of your skin. That was predestined. You did not choose the collection of genes and chromosomes that make up the person that you are. That was predestined. You had no opportunity to choose the country in which you were born or, perhaps, even the country of which you are presently a citizen.

If you are lying in a hospital, whether you are a victim of an accident or ill health, you most probably did not choose your situation. Whether you were born into poverty or wealth, you had no opportunity to choose your circumstances. There are many events—some tragic—over which we can exercise no control. When these befall you, remember this message: Choose the winning attitude! You may not choose the circumstances, but you can choose the attitude with which you react to them. And whatever you do, choose the winning attitude!

> I may not be able to choose my circumstances, but I can choose the attitude with which I react to them.

Transforming Power

"Mind not high things, but condescend to men of low estate. Be not wise in your own conceits."

Romans 12:16

Look and study very carefully your prejudices, your passions, and your concerns. Chances are, it will be in these areas that you will discover your blind spots. And we all have them. In other words, if you feel very deeply and passionately on some prejudicial issue, I would advise you to look at it very carefully and just play a game and take the other side of the coin. Try putting yourself in the other guy's shoes. You may be led into an area of your emotional life where growth and maturity are deeply called for.

Pray about these things now. Write down what you feel God has told you to do about them.

_____

_____

_____

_____

_____

> **I will put myself
> in the other guy's shoes.**

Transforming Power

"The Lord will work out his plans for my life—for your loving kindness, Lord, continues forever."

Psalms 138:8

God wants you to succeed. He made you and He's got a beautiful plan for your life. Affirmation of your belief in personal success is the first step toward a winning attitude. Say to yourself, "I want to succeed. I will succeed."

In a paper first published in 1915, Freud very wisely and correctly pointed out that there are people who actually are "fear seekers." Just when it looks like they will reach the pinnacle of success, they blow it. They make a wrong decision. They plant their feet firmly and refuse to move forward, to sign the contract, or take the challenge. The psychological explanation for this phenomenon would fill volumes, so the best I can do is give you a swift, therapeutic, healing technique to help you overcome this fear of success. That technique is the positive affirmation of your desire and will to succeed. Affirm to yourself that you will dare to succeed. You desire to succeed, because you deserve to succeed.

Practice positive affirmation. It works. When God created you, He gave you a subconscious and a conscious mind which will respond to this kind of treatment. Commit your way to the Lord and He will crown your efforts with success! A winning attitude starts with positive affirmation.

> **I want to succeed.**
> **I will succeed.**

283

Character-Building Power

"You are to live clean, innocent lives as children of God in a dark world."

Philippians 2:15

I was on a plane a while back and a man came and sat next to me. "Where do you live?" I asked. "Green Bay, Wisconsin," he answered. "Oh, I've heard of that," I said. "But what does Green Bay have outside of the Packers?" He said, "I don't know. As far as I'm concerned Green Bay, Wisconsin, is the Green Bay Packers. After all, I'm the coach." "How's your next season going to be?" I asked. He said, "Great." I said, "How can you be so sure?" "Because," he said, looking me in the eye, "we've got talent."

And I said to him, "What's talent?" He looked at me and finally retorted. "You know, I guess it's character. Young men that are basically clean and wholesome and good."

There is no substitute for strong moral fiber, if you want to be a super success. You can look at some people who are climbing pretty high up the ladder, and they may have a pretty rotten moral life. But believe me if they ever reach the top, everybody is going to look at them pretty closely. Their immorality will be exposed, and they're going to come falling down. You know, only the good, clean, moral, upright person dares to get to the top.

Supersuccessful people. I know a lot of them personally. I can tell you, it's not talent, unless you call talent character. The exciting thing about that is that character is something anybody can develop, with the help of Jesus Christ.

**Lord, help me develop good character
and dare to head for the top.**

Character-Building Power

"I have set before you life or death, blessing or curse. Oh, that you would choose life."

Deuteronomy 30:19

You can choose to be a blessing or you can choose to be the kind of a person who is a curse to those who have to live with you. "I have set before you life or death, therefore choose life."

The exciting thing about this is that everyone is given the power and the freedom, by God, to choose what kind of life he wants to live, what he wants to accomplish, and what he wants to achieve. It all begins with goal setting.

There is a better life for you if you will discover the principles for successful goal setting. Because ultimately where you are and where you will go depends upon what goals you have set or will set for yourself.

The secret of success is to set the right goals and never take your eyes off them.

Have you taken your eyes off your goal? Rewrite it down today.

———————————————————

———————————————————

Now, keep your eye on it!

> **I have set a goal and
> will keep my eyes on it.**

285

Character-Building Power

"But everyone knows that you stand loyal and true. This makes me very happy. I want you always to remain very clear about what is right, and to stay innocent of any wrong."
Romans 16:20

Your goals must be compatible with your own deepest value system. If they are not, you will have tension, guilt, and anxiety inside of you and you won't be able to succeed. At your deepest level you must ask yourself, what did I believe as a child? What were the deepest, purest, greatest ideals I ever looked up to? Perhaps today you've separated yourself from these great moral ideals that you once held. I say to you, in setting your goals—go back to your highest values and your highest ideals and make certain that whatever goals you are setting for yourself professionally, spiritually, or in any way, that they are compatible with these God-inspired ideals. If they are not, you won't be able to give it all you've got!

That's why ultimately only the honest man enjoys happy success. Make sure your goals harmonize with your value system. Then you will come to the end of your life with pride behind you, love around you, and hope ahead of you.

My value system will guide me.

Character-Building Power

"Best of all, they went beyond our highest hopes, for their first action was to dedicate themselves to the Lord and to us, for whatever directions God might give to them through us."
2 Corinthians 8:5

The other day my son and I attended the bar mitzvah of my dear friend Rabbi Brooks' son. It was a glorious experience. In the ceremony, the son gave a little sermonette he had written himself. "What is a bar mitzvah?" the young man began. "Is it a time for food and merriment and dance? Is it a time to listen to the special words of my father? Or does it mean that I have become a man? Perhaps. But to me bar mitzvah is two things: dedication and devotion to a dream."

Then the rabbi cupped his son's face gently in his hands, and they looked into each other's eyes. Standing before the entire congregation, the Rabbi spoke these words to his son: "My dream for you, my son, is that you shall be a man—a good man, and a God-fearing man." And with tears glistening in his eyes, the young son nodded his head, "Yes, Father," he said, "I shall always love God." I say that a bar mitzvah is the union of dreams—a father dreaming that his son will bring honor and glory to his family name and to his faith. And a son dreaming he will meet, and perhaps exceed, the expectations of his father.

> **I have dedication and devotion to my dream.**

Character-Building Power

"Many are the plans in a man's heart, but it is the Lord's purpose that prevails."

Proverbs 19:21

I spoke with a young man recently whom I have known for more than twenty-four years. I'd seen him grow from a child into an adult. "What are you doing these days, John?" I asked. "I'm just drifting," he replied. "I'm looking for God's guidance." Today he's twenty-eight years old. "How far did you go though college?" I asked. "College?" he began vaguely, "I think I was a junior when I dropped out." "Well what have you been doing since?" I pressed. "Well," he answered, "I worked in an autobody shop for a while. Then I tried selling some stuff for a salesman, but that didn't last long. Just recently I started going to a meditation class. I'm still going to classes and waiting for God to lead me." "Young man," I replied firmly, "I've known you almost since the day you were born and I feel that I can talk to you like a father to his own son. You must learn to live under a discipline if you want your life to take any kind of definite shape or direction." That's so true with each one of us. We must be under discipline. What discipline must you live under today to shape your life?

> **I will let discipline
> shape my life.**

Character-Building Power

"So, whether you eat or drink or whatever you do, do it all to the glory of God."

1 Corinthians 10:31

Affirm, Believe, Commit and then Dream. Keep picturing in your mind the finished success. Dreaming means keeping your hope alive. Mentally visualize what it can be like when you've finally made it.

Expect to succeed and then finish what you start. Learn to live under firm self-discipline. I once spoke with a multimillionaire Texan. "What is the secret of your success?" I asked. "As a young boy," he drawled, "my father said to me, 'Buy real estate and never sell it.' I followed his advice." Finish what you start.

Even I must live under the discipline of God's Word and of the denomination with which we are affiliated. I've found that the most difficult persons to deal with are those who have never had to live under a discipline of any kind. That can be very dangerous to personality development. Everyone must learn to live under some self-inflicted controls.

Affirm, believe, commit, dream, expect, finish, and finally, glorify God. St. Paul said, "Glorify God in all you do." The primary reason success is so wonderful is that it brings glory to God. The successful mother, the successful marriage, the successful business, the successful accomplishment of a divine dream is a marvelous witness to the goodness of God. "Commit your way to the Lord and He will crown your efforts with success."

> **I will seek to glorify God in all I do.**

Character-Building Power

"Commit everything you do to the Lord. Trust Him to help you do it and He will."

Psalms 37:5

    Supersuccess is not a matter of talent. It's character. It's not a matter of territory. It's what kind of a person you are. Some of you think it's a matter of gimmicks or tricks. You think you have to manipulate people. But that's wrong. You have to choose a winning attitude. It doesn't come easily or naturally. When you're down, you don't even want to win. You just want to give in to failure, to slide, to sleep. But in order to succceed, you must first affirm and then believe. Next you must commit your way to the Lord and you'll succeed. What does the word *Commit* really mean? There are many people in today's world who don't know. Commitment means that you eliminate and eradicate all possible alternatives. You close the book on all other options. That's what makes a supersuccess a supersuccess. He dreams, he makes decisions, he lays plans, he sets goals, and he goes away. He's so determined that he will not fail.

    What dream are you committed to today?

_____

_____

_____

**I will choose a
winning attitude.**

Achieving Power

"There is no condemnation now for those who are in Jesus Christ."

Romans 8:1

Achieving power comes from courage. When you have been relieved of your negative self-image and your guilt, you begin to see possibilities within yourself. Then what happens? Then you have the courage to admit you need help and take training. You begin to study and to learn.

Jesus Christ gives me the courage to face my faults. I'm not perfect! And I'm not sinless! And I'm making mistakes every day! So are you. But when we are liberated enough to tell the world that we do have sins and faults and we are going to work on them with the help of God, that's what gives us achievement power! Success is never certain: Failure is never final. There is never anybody who will win unless he looks at himself constructively, positively, and self-critically for improvement until he makes it.

Finish this sentence: I know I can and will improve my life by _____

_____

_____

> **It's better I do something imperfectly
> than to do nothing perfectly.**

Achieving Power

"But if you give yourself to the Lord, you and Christ are joined together as one person."

1 Corinthians 6:17

By success we do not mean never missing your goal. It is not uncommon for people, for instance, to set their goals so low that they never miss. They go through life and proudly tell themselves that they've never had a failure, when the truth is they never set goals that were risky enough to possibly miss. We like to say the best illustration of success is the pole-vaulter. He succeeds in his moment of failure. He keeps setting the bar higher and higher and higher. It is not until he knocks it down that he knows he is a success. He's gone as high as he can. At that point of time he is a success.

And so a person has never really succeeded until he has failed. Let's make another point and that is, by success we do not mean making millions of dollars. By success we do not necessarily mean in commercial terms. Success is a matter of developing great personality. And the most beautiful personality is one in which Christ lives beautifully.

Success is never certain:
Failure is never final.

Achieving Power

"And all things, whatsoever ye shall ask in prayer, believing, ye shall receive."

Matthew 21:22

Some people think too short; they think too small. Almost always the solution to the problem is to think longer or to think bigger or to think deeper. Their sights are too small.

May I repeat my favorite story? I can't think of anything that illustrates my point better than the story of the man fishing on the pier. A tourist came and watched him. When he caught a fish, he would get out a measuring tape and measure it. The little ones he would throw in his bucket. If they were over ten inches, he threw them back in the water.

The tourist couldn't stand it. "What's the big idea?" He asked. "You keep the little ones and you throw the big ones away! What's the meaning of all that?" The fisherman looked at him and said, "Well, my frying pan is only ten inches long!"

Think bigger. Almost always that's where you'll find the solution to your problems. Do so today. Think bigger and write down your new ideas:

_____

_____

_____

> **Failure doesn't mean God doesn't answer my prayers. It does mean that God has a better idea.**

Achieving Power

"Blessed is that man that maketh the Lord his trust."
Psalms 40:4

Check the success potential before you set your goal. You can almost always check whether an idea will be a failure or a success before you begin, by asking is it practical? Does it fill a vital human need? Can it excel? Can it inspire? Is it pace-setting? Can your idea really meet a need? Can it be inspirational? Can you package it in such a way that people will want it? Will it touch them emotionally? If you're the first with the most, you can't lose unless you don't have the nerve to move ahead.

In setting goals don't surrender leadership to problems. Keep a positive attitude toward problems when you set your goals. Never bring the problem-solving phase into the decision-making phase. Don't let your problems take command; let possibilities take command! If you don't make the decision until you solve the problem, by the time you make the decision, somebody else will have done it ahead of you. Furthermore, most problem solving and creative thinking never happens when you're in a phase of indecision. When you make the decision, make the plunge because it's a great idea and it would help God and other people! Then you know you've got to sink or swim. In that kind of situation, the breakthrough ideas will come.

> **I won't surrender leadership
> to my problems.**

Achieving Power

"I am with you; that is all you need. My power shows up best in weak people."

2 Corinthians 12:9

Two years ago I visited Persepolis. Persepolis is one of the most forsaken places on planet earth. It's in Persia (Iran as we know it today) midway between the Persian Gulf and Teheran. It is not much more than Death Valley, yet Persepolis was the power center of the world during the time of Cyrus I, Cyrus II and Cyrus III. What made Persepolis great?

POWER NEVER GRAVITATES TO PLACES.

POWER ALWAYS GRAVITATES TO PEOPLE.

Success is merely a study of the flow of power: Who gets power, how do they manage it, how do they control it, how do they restrain it? A supersuccessful person is a person with power. Power never flows to places, it flows to people.

Oh, Lord, nothing is impossible if we'll take Your power into our lives. Thank you, Jesus, for dreaming the impossible dream. You fought the unbeatable foe. Up Calvary's hill You bore the unbearable sorrow. You ran where brave men dared not go. And You did it to right the unrightable wrong. You loved pure and chaste from afar. When Your arms on that cross were so weary, You still reached the unreachable star. And the world is better for this. For my Lord, scorned and covered with scars, strove to His last ounce of courage, to reach the unreachable star. Amen.

God's Gifts to You

Faith

"Look, his soul is puffed up, it is not upright in him! But the righteous shall live by his faith."

Habakkuk 2:4

An immaculate faith—unstained, unsoiled, unspotted, unscarred by criticism, self-pity, ego-tripping, jealousy: where the motives are to help people who are hurting and to glorify God.

An immaculate faith—a faith that doesn't rise out of your own vain imaginations, but faith that has its tap roots in the very center and the core of God Himself.

An immaculate faith—the kind of faith that when it turns into a reality, makes the world more beautiful and your life more lovely. I suggest to you that this is the most precious quality that human life can ever achieve.

**Immaculate faith
makes the world more beautiful.**

Faith

"No servant can serve two masters; for either he will hate the one and love the other, or he will be devoted to one and despise the other. You cannot serve God and mammon."

Luke 16:13

There was a man who had three friends: two, he treasured highly; one, he did not care much about and was too busy to think about.

Then one day this man received a notice from his king that he was to be called into court. Fearfully, he called on his best friend, and the best friend said, "I'm sorry. I can't go with you." He went to the friend whom he treasured second best and this man said, "I'm sorry. I'll go with you to the palace gate, but that's as far as I'll go." Then he went to his third friend whom he had ignored and neglected too long. This friend said, "Oh, I will go with you. I think I can help you." That friend not only went with him, but went into the courtroom, stood up and pleaded his case before the king, and he was relieved of the charges!

That king is God. That man is every man. The call to come to court is death. The first friend is money. When you are dying, that friend cannot go with you. So you call on your next most treasured friend. That friend is your family. They will go with you to the palace gate but no farther. But the third friend is named Faith. That friend says, "Yes, I will go with you. And He walks with you through the gate right up to the King where you are received into the bosom of God. That is the friend that I want you to claim today. Claim Christ as your friend and you will never be sorry.

> **Faith carried me
> into the bosom of God.**

Faith

"Since we have such a huge crowd of men of faith watching as from the grandstands, let us strip off anything that slows us down or holds us back, and especially those sins that wrap themselves so tightly around our feet and trip us up; and let us run with patience the race that God has set before us."

Hebrews 12:1

What do I mean by an immaculate faith? I mean a faith that is drawn to God out of love for Him more than out of a deep selfish interest in what you need and want. I'm talking about the kind of immaculate faith that is a deep commitment to a beautiful dream that comes from God because He wants to help people who are hurting. So dreams that form an immaculate faith are not ego trips. They are deep desires to help humans who hurt.

You know people who have an immaculate faith. Their lives transcend the commonplace. They fulfill what we call the window prayer of our new Crystal Cathedral: "Lord, make my life a window for Your light to shine through and a mirror to reflect Your love to all I meet."

Pray now that God will give you a desire to help people who are hurting. Write down what He tells you to do.

_____

_____

> **Lord, make my life a window
> for Your light to shine through.**

Faith

"For because of our faith, he has brought us into this place of highest privilege where we now stand, and we confidently and joyfully look forward to actually becoming all that God has had in mind for us to be."

Romans 5:2

You can step on that road right now if you will reach out and put my hands in yours and yours in mine and say, "Jesus Christ, I want an immaculate faith, unstained by cynicism, unstained by self-pity and jealousy and arrogant doubt. Jesus Christ, I want to be a beautiful person, a window for Your light to shine through and a mirror to reflect Your love to all I meet. Receive my soul, Jesus Christ, redeem me, save me, fill me with Your love. I believe You are doing it and it feels great. Amen."

Now, that's the beginning. It's surely not the end. It's the portal, not the main auditorium. It's the entrance, not the high altar. It's the turning not the cul de sac. That's where I think some of you have to begin right now. If you want an immaculate faith, discover the experiences that happen when you stop telling God it's impossible. Begin now by having a connection to that immaculate Lord who lived and died and rose again!

**I can become the person
God wants me to be.**

Faith

"Consider it complete joy, my brothers, when you become, in all sorts of trials, well aware that his testing of your faith brings out steadfastness."

James 1:2,3

"Dear Abby" once told me of her husband's sister Helen, who had suffered polio as a young woman. "She's in a wheelchair but she can not even feed herself. She is such an exciting, enthusiastic, happy, buoyant person." I asked Abby, "What is her secret?" Abby said, "She always forgets about herself and thinks only about others. For instance she is very busy these days reading law books to a blind law student at the University. That is her whole life's project today." I said, "How can she read if she can't use her hands?" Abby told me, "She has this long object that she holds in her mouth to flip the pages as she reads. It won't be too many more months before this student will graduate from one of the top universities in the United States, a great lawyer, and he'll go out and help people solve their problems. And he will have gotten his education even though he was totally blind, because one woman read all his books to him."

Then Abby made this statement and I think it is one of the more beautiful sentences I have ever heard in my life. Abby said, "You know, Bob, no matter how handicapped you are, you can do something that somebody else cannot do."

Forget about yourself and think about others.

Faith

"And Jesus answered them, 'Truly, I say to you, if you have faith and never doubt, you will not only do what has been done to the fig tree, but even if you say to this mountain, 'Be taken up and cast into the sea, it will be done.' "

Matthew 21:21

How do you communicate with God? You communicate with God through prayer. And what is prayer? Prayer is a form of thinking. You don't use your teeth, you don't use your fingers, you don't use your knees, you don't use your stomach, you don't use your liver, you don't use your heart, you use your head and you think thoughts as you're talking to God. And if you think it's impossible, you're telling Him it's impossible. Miracles happen when you stop telling Him it's impossible. Get out of His way, and give Him a chance to work a miracle.

An immaculate faith is a commitment to a dream that comes from God. If it wasn't impossible from a human perspective, it wouldn't require faith at all. Faith is attempting to do the impossible for Him. An immaculate faith is a gift from God!

**God performs miracles when we
stop telling Him it's impossible!**

Confidence and Enthusiasm

"We work with you for your joy, for you stand firm in your faith."

2 Corinthians 1:24

You can make a commitment, but then you must have confidence. That's the second human value.

"Confidence, Lord, is flowing into me now. For my conscience is clear. I will face challenges calmly and serenely, for God is behind me all the way. He will help me. And if I must go through difficult times because of my commitment, He will rescue me. I feel His Spirit of confidence surging in my heart now. With Him I cannot possibly fail. I have a strong feeling that everything is going to work out just beautifully. Thank you, Lord. Amen."

Everything will work out beautifully.

Confidence and Enthusiasm

"Thou, O Lord, art a shield about me, my glory and the lifter of my head."

Psalms 3:3

I heard the story of a minister who was very low and had a very negative self-image. He was the senior minister of his church, and things obviously were not going right. In a very low time he entered the sanctuary, knelt at the altar, and prayed a very depressing negative, destructive prayer. He said, "Oh, God, I am nothing, I am nothing." Just at that point one of the assistant ministers opened the door and was very impressed by the senior minister's humility. So the assistant minister came in and knelt alongside the senior pastor and joined him in praying, "Oh Lord, I am nothing, I, too, am nothing." Whereupon the janitor happened to enter the auditorium and was awestruck by the humility of the ministers. Not to be outdone, he joined them as he knelt at their side and said, "Oh, Lord, I, too, am nothing, nothing, nothing." The assistant minister looked at the janitor and said to the senior minister, "Now look who thinks he's nothing!"

It's incredible, isn't it, how some people put themselves down and how even religion puts some people down. Some people think that if they put themselves down that this is humility! Not so! Anyone who has that concept of humility is not a Christian. It is a distortion of Christianity.

Lord, I am something!

Confidence and Enthusiasm

"What does it profit a man if he gains the whole world and loses his own soul?"

Matthew 16:26

Shortly before Jesus was crucified, He came through Jericho. The crowds jammed the streets, but there was one man, small of stature, who climbed up into a tree and clung to the branches so he could get a good look at Jesus. His name was Zacchaeus, and he was a tax collector—a traitor to his own people. Zacchaeus forfeited his patriotism to get money. He thought money would give him power and power would make him self-confident. But that wasn't the answer. The drive for confidence is really a hunger for God.

Jesus looked up at him and said, "Zacchaeus, make haste and come down. I must stay at your house today. Salvation has come to your house." Jesus knew what a sinner he was, but instead of giving him a sermon, He paid Zacchaeus a compliment. Zacchaeus found self-confidence when he was saved by Jesus Christ. At that time he gave half of his goods to the poor and restored fourfold all he had defrauded.

**Salvation has come
to your house!**

Confidence and Enthusiasm

"Be not conformed to this world but be transformed by the renewal of your mind."

Romans 12:2

You see somebody who is uptight, putting on a false front, driving for power and money and fame, and you can be sure that person suffers deep-seated insecurity. Some think that if they go along with the crowd, then they'll be popular and will feel secure and confident. But the moral level of the masses is always low. The moral value of the individual who stands above the crowd is exemplary.

Others pursue the quest in the realm of superstitions. It is unthinkable that in this day people with college degrees are falling for astrology. The emphasis on astrology, undue attention to demonology, etc., is a reversion back to superstitious hangovers of the most primitive, nonconstructive religion.

Don't look to the stars for confidence. Look to the Star, Jesus Christ. Be not concerned about what star you were born under. Be concerned about whether you are born again under The Star.

I have confidence! Let me tell you where I get it: God is my Father! Jesus Christ is my personal Savior! The Holy Spirit lives in me! And my confidence is built on the promise: "If God be for us, who can be against us?"

> **Don't look to the stars—
> look to The Star.**

Confidence and Enthusiasm

"But you shall receive power when the Holy Spirit has come upon you; and you shall be my witnesses in Jerusalem and in all Judea and Samaria and to the end of the earth."

Acts 1:8

You must know that enthusiasm is the very force of God coming within you. You know, the word *enthusiasm* comes from the two Greek words, *En theos*—in God. And that's why the most enthusiastic people I know are the people who have the Holy Spirit within them. They're turned-on people. They've actually got God inside of them.

So if you want enthusiasm, affirm, "I am enthusiastic." At first you will feel like a phony, and from the surface standpoint, you probably are. But you will be creating the genuine.

So tell your subconscious mind, "I am enthusiastic, I do love life. I do love my wife, I do enjoy living. I do believe in God." If you affirm these positive affirmations, the subconscious mind records them, and later on these affirmations come bubbling up, not in the verbalized form in which they were recorded, but in a vague form of a happy mood that you can't explain.

**Enthusiasm—don't block it!
Unlock it!**

Confidence and Enthusiasm

"Since we have a Great Priest over the house of God, let us draw near with a true heart in full assurance of faith."
                                        Hebrews 10:21,22

Believe that you can live a highly enthusiastic life. Believe that God can come within you and change and transform you.

Believe in the beauty of life as it is and as it can become. Some of you are not enthusiastic because your dreams have cracked and crumbled in your hands. Others aren't enthusiastic because they're not happy on the job, and still others because they've got a guilt deep within them. And God is over there someplace, you're over here and the chasm between is greater than the Grand Canyon, and you don't even want God to come any closer because you'd have to repent and make changes. And that, you don't want to do.

Obviously, my friend, if you hold a negative thought in your mind about God, your business, your faith, your religion, your church, your marriage, your wife, or your child, you are responsible for your own bad mood today. And you're not going to fix the problem until you fix the blame! If you are enthusiastic, think positively now and believe the beautiful life that God wants you to have!

Write down any negative thoughts you have right now and pray that God will take them from you.

_____

_____

I'll see it when I believe it!

Confidence and Enthusiasm

"Therefore, if anyone is in Christ, he is a new creation; the old has passed away, behold, the new has come."

2 Corinthians 5:17

God made man with the capability of responding emotionally, laughing, crying, and loving. God made you so that you have the capability of being emotional, because the emotion of enthusiasm is the Holy Spirit of God Himself coming inside of you to remake you.

The next time you go to the refrigerator to get an egg . . . I want you to remember this question: "Can an egg fly?" That's funny of course! Anybody knows an egg can't fly! Wait a minute . . . "Yes! An egg can fly if it is born again! When new life breaks out of the shell, wings come out!"

This is happening to you right now. There's a stirring within you. And what is it? It's God's Spirit saying to you, "Break out of your shell, and let me give you wings!"

**With God's wings,
I can fly!**

Courage and Perseverance

"Cast your bread upon the waters, for you will find it after many days."

Ecclesiastes 11:1

God will give you the courage to CARE.

Once a woman went to an orphanage and asked to adopt a child who nobody wanted. "She's ten years old," said the matron, "ugly and with a horrible hunchback. She is sickly and ill-tempered. Only her name is beautiful, Mercy Goodfaith."

Thirty-five years later, a report came into the state on one of its orphanages. "It is outstanding, clean, with wonderful food. This is attributable to the matron, whose soul oozes love. I dropped in one evening unexpectedly. After dinner, one girl played the piano and the children sang Christian songs. The matron sat in a big chair with two little girls on one arm and two on the other. The children sat on her lap and others hovered near. Never have I seen such beautiful eyes as in that matron. So beautiful that I almost forgot how ugly her face was and how gruesome was her hunchback. Her name was Mercy Goodfaith."

God will give you the
courage to care.

Courage and Perseverance

"Bear one another's burdens and so fulfill the law of Christ."
Galatians 6:2

Twenty-four years ago at the beginning of my ministry, I had no secretary. Lois Wendell, a new church member, came to me saying, "I'm not a secretary, but I'll help until you can find someone better." She and my wife were the people with whom I shared my dreams!

Two years later she developed cancer, and there were many days when she couldn't get out of bed. She would drop onto the floor and crawl into the bathroom where she would be sick until her whole body seemed destroyed. Then she would reach for the sink, pull herself up to her feet, and force herself to get dressed. She drove alone to this church and was always there before me. When asked, "How are you?" she always answered, "Great!" I never knew what she had just gone through.

Through the years she received daily phone calls from church members and Hour of Power viewers across the country. They would cry and complain about their problems, and she listened to it all. In her sickness she had courage to bear others' problems!

> **God will give you the**
> **courage to care.**

Courage and Perseverance

"Strengthened with might through his Spirit in the inner man."
Ephesians 3:16

I recall a missionary in India who told how he was kneeling at his bed praying one night when a giant python, not uncommon in that area, uncoiled itself from the rafters and wrapped itself around his body. "In quietness and confidence shall be your strength," the Bible says. And the missionary said he received strength from God to be so calm and so brave that he never moved. He just kept meditating. Had he struggled, had he hesitated, had he tensed up, the coils would have been constricted, and he would have been crushed. He prayed, he waited, he became calm, he remained poised, he didn't move, and after long minutes the snake uncoiled itself and retreated back to the rafters.

**God will give you the
courage to dare.**

Courage and Perseverance

"If you cling to your life, you will lose it; but if you give it up for me, you will save it."

Matthew 10:39

Once there was a helpless drunk who was brought into a New York hospital for the fiftieth time. A doctor there asked him to speak to a young boy of nineteen who had been brought in for the first time.

The old drunk looked at the young man and began to talk; "You don't want to turn out the way I did," he said, "I was young like you once, with hopes and dreams." The more he spoke to the boy the more he felt he had a mission in life. He had to save that boy! They talked all morning and finally made a promise. The old man said, "If you ever need a drink, you call me, okay?" And the boy answered, "I'll do the same for you."

That was the turning point for Bill, the founder of Alcoholics Anonymous. When he shared his life to save another, he himself was saved! He found the very power of God.

**God will give you the
courage to share.**

Courage and Perseverance

"Praying always with all prayer and supplication in the Spirit and watching thereunto with all perseverance and supplication for all saints."

Ephesians 6:18

What is the best thing that has happened to you in the past five years?

A market research firm was assigned by the *Wall Street Journal* to go out and ask this question, and twelve percent of the people gave exactly the same one-word answer: "Nothing."

What is the best thing that has happened to you in the past five years? If you said, "Nothing," that's your fault. Because, you see, the secret of dynamic and effective living is really up to you. It's a matter of making a commitment confidently, which means that you establish a long-range goal and objective. (Too many people have only a vague idea of what they might want to accomplish in their one lifetime.) Then once you've established a firm objective, you translate this objective into immediate steps, intermediate steps, long-range steps and ultimate steps. Once you've done this, all you need is perseverance to make it. And good things will happen to you!

Perseverance is that quality that makes it possible for you to live in such a spirit that nothing ever keeps you down.

Take a sheet of paper, and prayerfully set down some long-range goals.

**Good things
will happen to you!**

Courage and Perseverance

"No man having put his hand to the plough, and looking back, is fit for the kingdom of God."

Luke 9:62

Enrico Caruso was told by his first voice teacher, "Your instrument sounds like a raw wind whistling through a window." He did not listen to her. He persevered.

Marconi, who invented the wireless, said to his colleagues, "I think the discoveries of Heinrich Kurtz in Germany have paved the way for the possibility of developing wireless communication." And they said, "That violates all known laws of physics." He did not listen to them. He persevered.

My friend, Walter Burke, until recently the president of McDonnell-Douglas Corporation, was told while studying aeronautical engineering in St. Louis at the University, "A plane will never break the sound barrier. It's physically impossible. It would shatter to pieces, if you could invent an engine big enough to fly that fast." He didn't listen. He persevered.

Just don't listen to negative thinkers! Listen to positive thinkers!

Listen to positive thinkers!

Courage and Perseverance

"Be watchful, stand firm in your faith, be courageous, be strong. Let all that you do be done in love."

1 Corinthians 16:13,14

Do you know who was the most persevering person who ever lived? Jesus Christ, of course!

He set a goal for Himself, namely to die on the cross for our salvation. And when He got right down to the wire, the night before He was crucified, He sweat drops of blood in the Garden of Gethsemane. But He said, "Father, not my will but Thine be done." And He went through with it.

Many of you have made commitments that you're wavering about now. I say, keep your eye on the flag!

Some of you remember as I do that when the pioneers back in the midwest broke prairie country, they would walk up to the top of a hill, drive a stake, tie a flag on it, go to the bottom, put their plow in the ground, and keeping their eye on the flag, plowed until they got to it. And when they looked back, they had plowed a straight furrow.

Keep your eye on the flag! You'll make it! You'll be a great success with perseverance! I promise you!

Keep your eye on the flag!

Patience and Forgiveness

"Wait on the Lord: be of good courage, and he shall strengthen thine heart."

Psalms 27:14

The greatest power in the world has the power literally to shake the top of a mountain, carve it, and crumble it to bits. And the power that can churn a granite mountain into dust also has the power to come into a human heart, heal a wound, and change a soul. It is a power that you can tap; and it can make your dreams come true and change your destiny. The greatest power in the world is the power of TIME.

Patience puts power in your heart and dreams. You can become the person you want to be and you can succeed in a most phenomenal goal-setting plan, if you're willing to pay the price in terms of time. Almost anything can be accomplished by the patient man.

Inch by inch
anything's a cinch.

Patience and Forgiveness

"We can rejoice too, when we run into problems and trials for we know that they are good for us, they help us learn to be patient."

Romans 5:3

My friend, Pat Nordberg, had an aneurism in her brain. Brain surgery left her a wounded, mental cripple. Some time later she was in the nursery of her church and noticed a brain-damaged child who was being completely ignored. Pat, with her wounded mind, felt sorry for this little child. She put the little girl's head on her lap, and through that touch of love, the child broke down and cried. Pat thought, "Oh, God, if just loving a little brain-damaged child could help her this much, what could I do if I were a psychologist?" She decided then that God wanted her to become a child psychologist.

She enrolled in college and worked very hard, averaging only three hours of sleep at night! Still, her wounded mind could not retain what she read, so she had only a C average to begin with. But she would not quit!

Fourteen years after her surgery, Pat finally got her Master of Arts degree! Today she is one of the most therapeutic healing Christian child psychologists in the public school system!

Harness the pyramiding power of time!

Patience and Forgiveness

"For therein is the righteousness of God revealed from faith to faith: as it is written, The just shall live by faith."

Romans 1:17

"Wait on the Lord: be of good courage, and he shall strengthen thine heart," and give you the power to make your dream come true. What it requires, of course, is tremendous faith. Show me a man who has faith in God, and I'll show you a man who's got patience!

Some of you have to take the time limit off God. You pray your prayers, and God doesn't answer, so you say, "He doesn't answer prayer." But wait a minute! God doesn't say that He will answer you when you ask! Take the time limit off God! Take the ceiling off God!

I know that God has a better life for you. He has a beautiful plan for your future. He's simply waiting for you to become a possibility believer! But you're not going to become that kind of believer until you can think longer. No, you couldn't do it in a year, maybe not in five. But could you do it in twenty years? The mountain-moving power of the long look is what gives vision. And no power is greater than the power of a vision, a dream.

God saves His best gifts for
His most patient people.

Patience and Forgiveness

"If we confess our sins, He is faithful and just to forgive us our sins, and to cleanse us from all unrighteousness."

1 John 1:9

The word *love*, at its depth, really means forgiveness. Many of you are aware of the fact that there are three Greek words for love—*eros*, *philo*, and *agape*. *Eros* means love only in the sense of the sexual aspect. From it comes the word erotic. *Philo* is the word the Greeks use when they refer to platonic or human relationships on a respectful level. For instance, the word *philosophy* comes from the Greek words *philo* and *sophia*—love of wisdom. The word *agape*, which the Greeks developed, is a word unlike any other in any other language, (unless it would be the word *grace* in English). *Agape* means to love somebody, especially because they do not deserve it. And that's the kind of love that God has for us. That word *agape* really can be translated "to FORGIVE."

Love wears a crown, and in the crown of love are many jewels. One jewel shines brighter than all the others. The Crown Jewel in the crown of love is forgiveness.

The Crown Jewel is forgiveness.

Patience and Forgiveness

"While we were yet sinners Christ died for us."

Romans 5:8

Back in the fourteenth century, a monk announced to the people of his village that he was going to preach the greatest sermon he had ever preached on the love of God. When it was time for the sermon, everyone was breathlessly awaiting the discourse of the clergyman. Instead of mounting into the pulpit, he went to the candelabra, drew a long burning candle, and then walked high in the altar where a sculptured form of Christ was nailed to the crucifix in the chancel. He silently lifted the candle until the glow was right underneath one of the pierced hands, and he held it there, with his back to his congregation. Then he shifted and held the candle below the pierced opposite hand of Jesus. Then he dropped it and held it along the side where the spear had punctured. And then he dropped to his knees, in prayer, holding the candle so the candlelight glowed on the pierced feet of Jesus. And after a moment he stood and turned holding the candle before him so that the people could see the gentle and affectionate tears flowing out of his eyes, and he said to his congregation, "My beloved people, that is my sermon on the love of God for you."

Sacrificial love brings forgiveness.

Patience and Forgiveness

*"Your heavenly Father will forgive you if you forgive those
who sin against you; but if you refuse to forgive them, he will
not forgive you."*

Matthew 6:15

You must forgive. The only alternative is to brace yourself for being treated most judgmentally by your fellowmen.
The only person who doesn't have to forgive is the person
who will never commit any sins. We are not perfect and we
need to be forgiven ourselves.

We need to forgive because we cannot have success, joy,
prosperity, physical health, or happiness without it. If you're
down, I would dare believe that the odds overwhelmingly
would prove that if you went into depth analysis, you'd find
that someplace in your life, right now, there lingers, in some
remote drawer in that closet of a corridor of your brain,
some guilt that has not been forgiven.

Pray now and ask God to reveal to you the people in your
life whom you have not forgiven. Now pray that He will
give you the grace to forgive each one.

I will forgive others.

Patience and Forgiveness

"For I will forgive their iniquity, and I will remember their sin no more."

Jeremiah 31:34

An esteemed clergyman in England told J. Wallace Hamilton, "The turning point came in my life when I was seventeen years old. I was called the black sheep in the family. We were always fighting each other. One night they were all picking on me: my mother, my father, my brother, and my sister, until I could not stand it anymore. I jumped up and cried, 'I'm leaving, I'm getting out of here.' I ran up the stairs and there suddenly in the darkened hallway, I ran into my grandmother. She had listened to it all. The diatribes, the accusations, the vilifications. She just stood in the hallway and stopped me by putting her hand on my shoulder. With tears in her eyes she said the words that changed my life. 'John, I believe in you.'"

And right now, can't you see Him? Stopping you in the middle of your tracks, coming down from the cross with a scar in His palm, as He puts His hand on your shoulder and says, "I've heard everything, but I want you to know, I believe in you."

Let Christ love you and He'll forgive you and save you.

What a great moment that is! You'll then become a forgiving person too!

I believe in you.

Peace

"Mercy and truth are met together; righteousness and peace have kissed each other."

Psalms 85:10

There was a Jewish lad who, as a young boy, decided to make a list of the great values he would pursue in his lifetime. He listed fame, he listed fortune, and he listed health. When he completed his list, he gave it to the rabbi who scanned it quickly, looking for one particular word, which he did not see. He said to the little boy, "You have missed one of the most important values of life, and that is peace of mind. What good is money, what good is fortune, what good is fame if you do not have peace at the core of your life?"

The Jewish people today still have this same greeting, "Shalom"—meaning peace. It was customary in the days of Jesus to greet each other with that wonderful greeting.

Shalom—Peace to you!

Peace

"He will keep in perfect peace all those who trust in Him whose thoughts turn often to the Lord."

Isaiah 26:3

A friend of mine who traveled the Atlantic many years ago tells this story: "One time our ship was caught in one of the terrible Atlantic storms in the wintertime. The ship seemed as if it were going to be ripped apart and split at the seams. It went on for days until one night it reached its peak and mob panic was about to break out. At that point the captain began to describe the ship's history: 'This ship has gone through many storms far worse than this one.' After he finished describing the ship and the storms it had encountered, he said in a strong confident voice, 'So! We will trust this good ship and God who rides the storm. And we will see it through!' And everyone felt at peace."

Prayer is the ship that can take you through the storm. Prayer has taken many a person through many a more violent storm than you're going through.

> **Board that ship called prayer and
> God will see you through.**

Peace

"Watch the upright and observe the righteous, for there is a future to the man of peace."

Psalms 37:37

Most people with troubled hearts have one simple problem: a guilty conscience.

You cannot have peace of mind if you're in hostility with God or your neighbor. If you have a troubled heart, if there is within you an unceasing disquiet and discontent, a nameless, indefinable tension, I ask you, are you really clean before God?

God has written a moral law in the universe. You have the freedom to ignore it, laugh at it, scorn it, or smash it. But in the final analysis, you do not break moral laws. In the final analysis, moral laws break you!

Live right. If you want to have peace of mind, live in such a way that when you come to the end of the day, you can look into the face of God in your bedtime prayers and not be embarrassed.

Live Right!

Peace

"Depart from evil, and do good; seek peace, and pursue it."
Psalms 34:14

Dr. Viktor Frankl, a man who has been an influence in my life, particularly through his writings and his lectures, is today the head of the Department of Psychiatry in Vienna, Austria, the position that Freud once held. Viktor Frankl is a Jew. During the Second World War, he was captured by the Nazis, and he tells how he was brought into a concentration camp. They took his cap, his shirt, his belt, and his shoes. Then they took his trousers and his underclothing until he was naked before them. Then they all laughed. After they had their laugh, they shaved him of all his hair. Then they took his watch and even his wedding ring. They took everything, looked at him naked, and they laughed. But in his mind, this is what Viktor Frankl thought: "There is one thing you have not robbed me of and that you cannot take. You cannot take from me my power and freedom to choose my attitude." And they never did. He suffered through those years in the concentration camp, but never did they take from him his power and freedom to choose his attitude. Out of it he became stronger than ever, with his great new psychological concept now called Logotherapy. Fantastic!

**I have the freedom
to choose my attitude.**

Tap Into Trust

Take the Trust Test

*"Trust in the Lord, and do good; so you will enjoy security.
Take delight in the Lord and he will give you the desires of
your heart."*

Psalms 37:3,4

This month you will discover a force that can transform
your life unlike any other. It is a positive quality that has recently demanded a great deal of psychological attention.
And rightly so, for as you'll soon find out, it's a spiritually
uplifting element that will add a new plus to your life.

What is it? It is the emotional and spiritual quality called
trust.

Trust—the spiritually enlightening element of historic
Christianity. Yet only recently has it caught the eye of the
trained psychologist. For years many people have confused
trust with gullibility. Cynics even today believe that to be
smart you must be skeptical.

What do you think? Is it smart or dumb to be a trusting
person? Look carefully at people you meet today.

> **I am about to discover
> a new thrust—trust!**

Take the Trust Test

"You shall know the truth and the truth shall set you free."
                                                    John 8:32

Is it smart or dumb to be a trusting person? Yesterday you asked that of yourself. The magazine *Psychology Today* recently asked this same question in an article entitled, "Trust and Its Consequences."

Dr. Julian Rotter of the University of Connecticut spent years studying the consequences of trust on human behavior and personality development. He then developed a scale to determine levels of trust in a person's life in comparison to their level of ten in behavioral patterns.

Based on his report, I've created my own true-false "Trust Test." Here it is:

1. True or False: Trusting persons tend to be more gullible.
2. True or False: Trusting persons tend to have a lower I.Q.
3. True or False: Trusting persons live happier lives.
4. True or False: Trusting persons tend to be more trustworthy.

Answers: 1-False; 2-False; 3-True; 4-False. Based on this test, how has your view of trust changed?

I'm going to be a smarter person—
I'm going to be a trusting person!

Take the Trust Test

"Jesus said unto him, 'If you can believe, all things are possible to him who believes.'"

Mark 9:23

According to psychologists, trusting persons live happier lives. As they tend to be better people in doing good, they are less likely to fall for a con. It's amazing but true! What it boils down to is this . . .

As birds were created to fly, and fish were created to swim, the human being was created to trust!

In our natural healthy state of mind, we were created to trust. A trusting person is a healthy person. A body that is healthy is functioning properly, whereas a body that is sick is not functioning properly. Therefore, the nontrusting person is sick. He is literally, "disfunctioning." The trusting person is functioning properly.

With this definition, the question arises: Why did God create the human being to be a trusting person? After all, isn't trusting taking a chance? What is God's reason behind the scheme of trust?

Think this through today. And as you do, ask yourself— how healthy are you? Are you functioning properly? Are you trusting God and those around you?

I am on the road to total health—
I am functioning in total trust.

Take the Trust Test

"Behold, God is my salvation, I will trust and not be afraid."
Isaiah 12:2

Why did God create you and me in such a way that when we have trusting natures our possibilities will evolve and develop? Why did God create the human being so that we are normal when we have faith and abnormal when we are dominated by doubt?

There is a thrust behind the trust, for all kinds of divine and God-created human energies are released when we break through the clouds of skepticism and stand in the sunlight of trust. God's system of living requires trust. You can survive and endure life without it, but you can't really enjoy life until you learn to live by trust.

**I am learning to
really enjoy life!**

Take the Trust Test

"Trust in the Lord with all your heart and lean not unto your own understanding. In all your ways acknowledge Him and He will direct your paths."

Proverbs 3:5,6

When someone trusts, tremendous forces are released. I believe that a trusting person is a persistent person. The person who is basically a nontrusting skeptic and doesn't live by trust, gives up quickly. Why has God created the system so that we have to trust? It's simple. He knows that trust releases enormous forces.

When you begin to trust God, you discover a real power. For when you realize that God believes in you and trusts you, then you begin to trust yourself. You have all kinds of powers of self-confidence to trust others and the ideas that God brings into your life. When someone trusts you, they help bring out the best in you. God trusts you because you are His child and you are created in His image. When you trust Him, He releases His tremendous power within you.

**I am God's Child—
and He trusts me!**

Take the Trust Test

"Like an eagle that stirs up its nest, flutters over its young, spreading out its wings, catching them."

Deuteronomy 32:11

Trust in God's scheme of throwing us out of the nest until we have to learn to fly. There's a great verse in the Bible that says, "Like an eagle that stirs up its nest, flutters over its young, spreading out its wings, catching them ..." Deuteronomy 32:11.

The thrust behind the trust is very simple. When you have to stand on your own two feet with no guarantee that the government or anyone else will rescue you, then you have to trust your own capabilities that the Creator God built within you.

Trusting persons become adventuring people, and adventuring people discover that when they take a chance together with God, excitement occurs. As energy is produced and success is realized, then the ultimate prize is in store. They realize, "I am an individual."

I am an individual!

Take the Trust Test

"He is my refuge and my fortress: my God; in Him will I trust."

Psalms 91:2

Ask yourself some questions:

Question 1: Do I believe that it is normal for me to be a trusting person and abnormal to be dominated by doubt?

Question 2: Am I satisfied with my level of trust or do I need to tap more of the tremendous power of persistence and positive perseverance?

Question 3: When have I acted on trust and perseverance and successfully achieved what I hoped for?

Question 4: After understanding God's trust in me, what is my response to the cross of Jesus Christ?

Question 5: As I trust God and believe that He has a plan for my life, I can trust myself and will begin to make the following decision, or take these steps of faith:

> **I have a lot to learn about trust.**
> **I have learned a lot already!**

The Thrust of the Trust

"The righteous man shall flourish like the palm tree and shall grow like a cedar in Lebanon."

Psalms 92:12

What is the thrust behind God's scheme of trust? The answer is found as we look at the two basic types of persons.

There are the "individuals" and the "invalids." As you look at all establishments—religious, political, economic, or social, you see they are made of people who either lean toward individualism or toward invalidism.

Invalidism is a system that keeps a person from discovering his own potential. An invalid is a sick person who is not functioning properly. Lack of trust produces and promotes invalidism.

Individualism is a system that allows healthy persons to develop the potential God has placed within them. An individual is glorifying and worshipping God by becoming the person God meant him to be.

Self-confident, redeemed persons are individuals—not invalids!

I will grow healthy—
I will grow trustworthy.

The Thrust of the Trust

"Bring the full tithes into the storehouse, that there may be food in my house, and thereby put me to the test, says the Lord of Hosts, if I will not open the windows of heaven for you and pour down for you an overflowing blessing."

Malachi 3:10

Because God wants us to be individuals, He created the trust system. The trust system produces individuals out of invalids.

The ultimate invalid is the newborn infant. Erik Erikson has taught us that in the first stage of a child's life, from birth to twelve months, the infant learns only one thing, and that is trust. I don't suppose there is a premature ward in a hospital today where nurses are not taught to stroke and talk to the premature infant to communicate trust. This therapy is based on Erikson's teaching that the newborn infant is born nontrusting. Birth is a traumatic experience and the infant must learn to live detached from the womb as an individual.

With this understanding, we can go so far as to say that we can measure immaturity and infantilism by the lowness of a person's capacity to trust.

You can measure the maturity and adulthood of a human being by the level that he reaches in his capacity to trust.

> **Trust is making me
> more of an individual.**

The Thrust of the Trust

"Trust in the Lord and do good, and He will give you your heart's desires."

Psalms 37:3,4

What do you really desire? Deep down in your heart you do not want to feel totally dependent on others. Trust makes all the difference in the world.

When you follow God's scheme of trust, you turn an invalid into an individual. You begin to do the impossible and obtain your heart's desire—freedom. You become free from dependence on others. That's the thrust behind the trust.

God pushes you out in faith so that you will discover what you can do and can be as an individual.

God will give you an idea that will challenge you to live by trust. The thrust behind the trust is God's way of preparing you to live for bigger and better things.

**I desire to do greater
things for God!**

The Thrust of the Trust

"I will go before you and make the crooked places straight."
Isaiah 45:2

Look carefully at the setup of our world today. These are entire systems that exploit the human being's natural desire to remain an invalid. Many political, social, and even religious, institutions exploit the nontrusting person by offering so much security that they won't have to face risk or danger.

The problem is this only perpetuates invalidism. In this setup, people really don't need to develop trust. Political promises offer to take care of them from the cradle to the grave. Even some forms of Christianity are inaccurate in turning their religion into a hospital instead of a physical fitness center.

When I was a child, I learned to love this hymn:

> Be not dismayed, whate'er betide,
> God will take care of you;
> Beneath His wings of love abide,
> God will take care of you.

This is good theology when understood in the right context, but if distorted, people simply think God will take care of them. Yet the song says, "Beneath His wings of love abide." This means beneath the wings of God's love, we can go out, take a chance, and run the risk.

I will take a chance!!

The Thrust of the Trust

"I will give you as a light to the nations, that my salvation may reach to the end of the earth."

Isaiah 49:6

Skepticism is all through the world and it affects your attitude toward God. Someone said to me, "If there is a God like you say there is, Schuller, why doesn't He come down and let us see Him?" I said to him, "He did . . . in Jesus Christ." "But," he argued, "That was 2000 years ago. Why isn't He fair about it and come down in our generation and every generation?" I said, "Come on now, look at the cross. He came down once, and once was enough. Think about it. You wouldn't want Jesus Christ to be crucified on a cross generation after generation. Trust Him—once is enough!"

Tremendous forces are released in the person who has learned to live believing that it can work.

The cross means trust. God trusts you and me enough to send His Son to die on the cross. If God didn't trust that the human race would respond to the cross, then He wouldn't have given the life of His Son, Jesus Christ. But God trusts that you will respond in faith, trust Him, and accept the salvation of Jesus Christ.

I believe in the cross!

The Thrust of the Trust

"Trust in the Lord forever."

Isaiah 26:4

"Trust in the Lord and do good . . . and He will give you the desires of your heart."

Psalms 37:3,4

Ask yourself some questions:

Question 1: Do I believe it is smart or dumb to be a trusting person?

Question 2: Am I satisfied with my level of trust, or do I need to take steps to raise my trust level?

Question 3: Am I aware of when I am responding to invalidism, or do I naturally allow systems to exploit and perpetuate this inclination?

Question 4: After understanding God's desire for me to be a trusting individual, am I meeting this challenge by taking risks?

Question 5: What step of faith, what risk, or what decision will I make today?

I trust You, Lord.

The Thrust of the Trust

"He will answer all my prayers."

Psalms 6:9

"Trust in the Lord and do good . . . and He will give you the desires of your heart." What is your heart's desire? There is nothing greater than being able to walk tall, relaxed, and confident as you face sun and rain, sickness and health, poverty and prosperity.

I invite you to understand the thrust behind the trust. I invite you to make a decision to do something risky. God wants you to discover the bigger and better life. You can have that when you learn to live the normal life, the life of faith.

Maybe you still need to take that first childhood step of trust. You need to turn from invalidism to individualism. You need to trust God. It was God who created the birds to fly, the fish to swim, and you to be a believer. People often say to me, "If God wants me to believe in Him, why doesn't He let us see Him?" My answer is, "He has, Jesus Christ." Jesus Christ is God taking form, as solid as the sun, as bright as a light, and as cheerful as the Holy Spirit. I invite you to take the first step of trust. Accept Jesus Christ and give your life to Him. It's daring, it's risky, and it's a commitment, but it's the first step to the ultimate life, the life of faith!

**My life is a life of faith—
nothing could be greater!**

Trust Means "Let Go and Let God"

"For we walk by faith, not by sight."

2 Corinthians 5:7

Tom Sullivan shared this with me. "When I was growing, Dr. Schuller, I was so angry about being blind that I didn't have time for God. My wife, Patty, always had a very strong faith, but mine didn't come until we very nearly lost our child.

"One day Patty had gone shopping and I was swimming in the pool with our little five-year-old girl. When the phone rang, I picked up the child and took her out of the pool. After hanging up, I heard a quiet little splash and knew she was in the water. I felt totally helpless as I thrashed in the water, calling her name. Finally I stopped still in desperation and said, 'Look, God, I haven't turned to You very often, but just give me one chance to save this child and I'll pay you back.' And then I heard a tiny, little sound . . . her air bubbles coming to the surface. I followed those bubbles and found her in about eight feet of water. She is alive today and very healthy.

"I feel that my blindness is a testimony to that old phrase, 'God helps those who help themselves.' I had to decide to be independent, to care about myself and to believe that anything is possible."

> Lord, Your strength shows up best in my
> weaknesses. Thank You for undergirding
> me with Your power.

Trust Means "Let Go and Let God"

"Blessed is the man who trusts in the Lord and has made the Lord his hope and confidence."

Jeremiah 17:7

You can enjoy living, but not until you learn to let go and let God handle your life. It's these three areas of life that can get you down. First, the stresses of life. Then the sins of life. And finally the successes of life. And I've had experience in all these areas, so I know what I'm talking about. I want to give you three sentences that you'll want to remember.

Let God's care handle your stress.

Let God's cross handle your sins.

Let God's control handle your success.

Lord, leaning on Your love liberates me and lifts me to triumphant living.

Trust Means "Let Go and Let God"

"Commit everything you do to the Lord. Trust him to help you do it and he will."

Psalms 37:5

Let go and let God! Leave your stress to God's care, leave your sins to God's cross, and leave your success to God's control and you're on your way to living with a capital L-I-V-I-N-G! I don't care who you are, where you come from, or what your problem is: Surrender your stress to His care, your sins to His cross, and your success to His control.

What are the stresses of life? Some of the stresses are failures. But God can turn your failures into successes, and you learn from them. Some of you today have an exciting dream, but you are afraid you're going to fail. Don't give up, rather, surrender to God. God is more interested in your success than you are. If you are His child, He doesn't want to see you fall flat on your face. He wants to give you success.

Write a short prayer below surrendering your dreams to God!

_____

_____

_____

**God turns my stress
into success!**

Trust Means "Let Go and Let God"

"And when you draw close to God, God will draw close to you."

James 4:8

Who are you? Does anybody know your name? Does anybody care about you? If you think that rising to the top of the ladder makes a difference, it doesn't. A few years ago, I took a taxicab from the Disneyland Hotel to my home, and we passed this magnificent church with the Tower of Hope and the Cross on top. Because of the exposure on television and in national magazines, I was sure the cab driver knew what this building was. So seeking praise in total modesty, I said, "What's the big building with the cross on top over there?"

And he said, "Oh, that's a Catholic hospital."

I was shocked. I asked, "How long have you been driving a cab here in Orange County?"

He said, " Eighteen years." I couldn't believe it. He lived right here for eighteen years and didn't know who we were. He didn't know who I was, and I'm sure he doesn't know who you are. That's one reason why people are discouraged and depressed. How do you handle it? With a dynamic faith!

Today I'm offering you a new way of living. It's held in these words, "LET GO AND LET GOD."

**Faith uplifts me
and gives me hope.**

Trust Means "Let Go and Let God"

"The kingdom of God is within you."

Luke 17:21

You probably need the nerve to make some drastic changes. You need what I have, and what a lot of people have, and that is a relationship with God. You need faith. You think nobody cares. You live in the kind of society today where nobody knows your name. It's easy to wonder, *Who am I, and does anybody care?*

When I begin to feel that way, I mentally gear up. I talk to myself and say, "I'm connected with the largest corporation in the world. It's the church of Jesus Christ. The International Christian Enterprise makes the biggest corporation look like peanuts and I'm proud to be part of it."

I'm proud to be a citizen
in the kingdom of God.

Trust Means "Let Go and Let God"

"I am leaving you with a gift—peace of mind and heart. And the peace I give isn't fragile like the peace the world gives."
John 14:27

What do you do with stress? You surrender it to His care. Your failures, your griefs, your setbacks, your insecurities, your feelings of inferiority—surrender them to His care.

You surrender your stress to His care and your sins to His cross. Did you know that the number-one psychological subconscious cause of stress is guilt? There is no way of dealing with guilt short of spiritual experience. I am all for psychiatry. I am all for psychology. I have studied both and still do. It's a continuing discipline for me, and I am not un-learned in this area. I commend every psychologist and psychiatrist, and in this church we have professionals in that realm. However, only the psychologist who has scars in His palms has the power to say to you, "I know what you have done. I forgive you." His name is Jesus Christ. He alone has the power to forgive and it is His cross. Surrender your stress to God's care, and your sins to God's cross.

> When I linger at the cross of Christ, He lifts
> my stressful burden . . . His yoke is easy.
> His burden is light.

Trust Means "Let Go and Let God"

"Your attitude should be the kind that was shown to us by Jesus Christ."

Philippians 2:5

Let go of your success to God's control. Would it surprise you that many people fear success more than failure? They do. I have had to do a lot of counseling trying to convince people that they ought to succeed, and that there is no sin in being a success. You don't have to feel guilty if you make a lot of money. Not at all. In fact, John Wesley said it years ago. "Make all the money you can. Save all the money you can. Then give all the money you can."

**Being able to help others is
God's idea of success.**

Trust Means "Let Go and Let God"

"The good man out of his good treasure brings forth good."
Matthew 12:35

No executive has a money problem. No person has a money problem. It's always an idea problem. If you need money, all you need are the right ideas. Money will flow to the right ideas, and success will come naturally and beautifully. A lot of people will benefit from success. Set success as your goal, for it's not a selfish objective. We need a lot of new thinking in America today. Success is not selfish; failure is. To choose to fail means that somebody's going to get hurt. Profit is a noble motive. If you don't have it, you'll be going out of business. It's just a matter of time.

> **God is the original self-giver.**
> **When I follow His lead, triumph follows.**

Trust Means "Let Go and Let God"

". . . I believe nothing can happen that will outweigh the supreme advantage of knowing Jesus Christ my Lord."

Philippians 3:8

Let me tell you something. I thank God that the church is a success, because that gives us power to help people who are really hurting. Let go and let God take care of your stress; let God's cross take care of your sins; and let God's control take over your success. You know what? You will find an inner fulfillment and you'll realize what I've been trying to say all the time. Life really can be sensational!

**In Christ,
my life is sensational!!**

Trust Means "Let Go and Let God"

"Happy is the man who finds wisdom and understanding for the gain from it is better than gain from silver and its profit better than gold!"

Proverbs 3:13,14

The secret of success is to have the best and the first and to be up front. If you want to succeed personally, corporately, or in a family way, you have to LET GO AND LET GOD run your life and business. I shared with the executives at the dedication how to be a success. It's really very simple. All you have to do is learn how to manage ideas. Some of you are experts in financial management. Some of you are experts in education, and some at driving trucks, cars, or taxicabs. I am an expert at something. I've developed a science of how to manage ideas. It's theological, psychological, and spiritual. It's letting go and giving control to God.

Success is God's idea so He manages *all* of my life.

Nest, Test, Invest, Arrest, and Crest

"It is the glory of God to conceal a thing. And it is the glory of kings to search things out."

Proverbs 25:2

Every idea goes through one of five phases. First there is the NESTING PHASE. The idea drops into your mind. Psychologists have discovered that the average brain has at least 10,000 ideas pass through it in a single day. That's incredible. But what really matters is whether they are positive or negative.

Studies show that for the average person 90 percent of all thoughts and ideas that pass through his or her mind are negative. Only 10 percent are positive! No wonder people are depressed or discouraged if 90 percent of their thoughts are negative. But the Stone Brandel Center found a small group of people with a remarkable difference. In this case, 75 percent of their daily thoughts were positive. Only 25 percent were negative. When they checked out the reason, they found that these positive people were basically religious people. They started the beginning of the day with a prayer. "Thank you, God." Their first thought was positive, and the last thought before they went to sleep at night was positive. It was a prayer. They were also attracted to Christian people and socialized with Christians. Positive thoughts dominate and attract.

> Positive, wholesome ideas permeate my mind when
> I listen to the quiet voice of God.
> He brings joy to others and to me.

Nest, Test, Invest, Arrest, and Crest

"In the morning sow your seed, do not let your hand lie idle in the evening. For which will prove successful you cannot tell; and it may be that all will turn out well together."

Ecclesiastes 11:6

In the NESTING PHASE, when the idea drops into your mind, in most cases an idea at this phase will probably die. George Petty said that had he not tuned in to the Hour of Power, the idea of an $80 million project would have died then and there. Lots of great ideas die in the nesting stage. Rather than lose terrific thoughts you can keep them alive from the nesting phase to the TESTING PHASE.

Here you can test the idea as positive or negative. Is it a constructive thought or creative dream? You simply have to ask the right questions. Would it be a great thing for God? Would it be a great thing for our country? Would it be a great thing for others around me?

Lord, give me positive ideas that will bring happiness and triumph to others as well as myself.

Nest, Test, Invest, Arrest, and Crest

"Consecrate them in the truth; your word is truth."
                                        John 17:17

As the nesting phase moves to the testing phase, you don't ask whether this idea is going to be assured success. You also don't ask if there is risk involved. Risk is involved in every great idea. There is no such thing as a *risk-free* society.

From the nesting and testing phase, the idea goes to the INVESTING PHASE. If it passes the positive test, then you make the commitment. Here is where you put your prestige on the line. You must run the risk of failure. You can be sure that someone may come and compete against you.

**Sailing on the growing edge of risk
brings triumph when God is at the helm.**

Nest, Test, Invest, Arrest, and Crest

"The kingdom of heaven is like leaven which a woman took and hid in three measures of meal till it was all leavened."
                                                        Matthew 13:33

I have a friend, Lillian Dixon, who's close to ninety years of age. She married her husband when he graduated from Princeton Seminary. Together they agreed to go and spend the one life they had for the work of God where the need was greatest. So they got on a boat, went to Formosa, and the first thing they did was to go and see a government official. He listened as they shared how they wanted to help the people in Formosa with schools and hospitals and churches. Finally he said, "Look, young people, you're both in your twenties, very young, and very idealistic. But there is no way you can do anything here in Formosa." He explained. "Look at that ocean. If you take a bucket of water out of the ocean, it doesn't make any difference. You can spend your life here, and it's like taking a bucket of water out of the ocean. The needs are too great. Please go back to America."

Lillian Dixon said to him in her fiery ladylike way, "Well, then if that's the case, I'm just going to fill my bucket! The ocean may not know the difference, but the bucket will."

That was over fifty years ago. Her husband has since passed away, but at last count, Lillian has established over 1,000 hospitals, schools, and churches.

> **Only God knows how many apples
> are in one seed.**

Nest, Test, Invest, Arrest, and Crest

"Be still and know that I am God."

Psalms 46:10

From the nesting phase, through the testing phase, the idea comes to the investing phase when you put in the risk capital. If it passes this phase, it goes on to the ARRESTING PHASE.

The nesting phase, the testing phase, the investing phase, the arresting phase all lead up to the CRESTING PHASE.

As you reach the top of the mountain, the idea becomes something beautiful. Whether it's a cathedral, a paper plant, or a thousand jobs, the idea becomes something fantastic.

Do you want to live an exciting life? Do you want to be productive and positive? LET GO AND LET GOD THINK THROUGH YOUR MIND.

"Be still and know that I am God" (Psalms 46:10).

Lord, your glorious mountain-top experiences
make even my valleys beautiful.

Nest, Test, Invest, Arrest, and Crest

"But blessed are your eyes for they see and your ears, for they hear."

Matthew 13:16

What is your idea? The nesting phase can kill it. It could die in the testing or investing phase. Even the arresting phase could let it die very easily. But consider the cresting phase. Let God think His thoughts through your mind. And as He opens the creative channels to let your dream live, you'll have a fantastic surprise waiting down the road.

Write your dream on the lines below:

_____

_____

_____

_____

_____

_____

_____

_____

Jesus Christ gives me a dream, He keeps my dream alive. He brings it to successful reality!

The Miracle of Love's Rewards

Love Conquers Fear

"There is no fear in love, for perfect love casts out fear."
                                                    1 John 4:18

Wouldn't it be wonderful if something happened deep within your mind to give you such inner confidence, security, and calmness that you would never be afraid of anyone or anything ever again? Wouldn't it be fantastic if you had a mental and spiritual experience that would permanently give you an imperishable and invisible shield against anxiety, worry, fear, and guilt?

The truth is if you have an experience with "perfect love," you will conquer fear in your life forever.

It is important to understand there is "imperfect love" as well as "perfect love." All doctrines, lectures, sermons, messages, books, and songs refer to "imperfect love." That's part of the problem with the world today. Much of what we think of as love is "imperfect love." Consider there are three levels of love:

1. *"I love you because I need you."* This is basically a selfish love and is imperfect.

2. *"I love you because I want you."* Could be nothing more than lust.

3. *"I love you because you need me."* This is what I call "Christian love," because it is the kind of love that Jesus showed.

Look at those around you and see if they have needs that you can do something about. Think of one thing you can do today for someone.

> **Christ, help me to be aware of
> the needs of others.**

Love Conquers Fear

"Yes indeed, it is good when you truly obey our Lord's command, 'You must love and help your neighbors just as much as you love and take care of yourself.'"

James 2:8

No human being is totally perfect in love, but Christ is. Let's suppose you run into somebody you can't love. What do you do? A friend of mine, Frank Laubach, taught me a lesson. He said, "Put one hand up in the air, open your palm and reach the other hand out, with a pointed finger aimed at your adversary. Now pray, 'Jesus Christ, You are perfect love. I am imperfect love. And because I'm imperfect, I can't love that person.' (Keep your finger pointed at him or her. Aim at the heart.) Continue praying, 'Let Your love fall into the palm of my hand, flow down through my arm, through my elbow, through my pointed finger, and hit his heart, please. Hit him with Your love, Lord. You love Him, Jesus! You can do it! And I will allow You to love Him through me.'"

There is a hymn that closes with the lines, "The love of Jesus, what it is, none but His loved ones know." It's not something you can be *taught,* it has to be *caught.*

> **Lord, I give You permission to use me
> to love all those my life will touch today!**

Love Conquers Fear

"Most important of all, continue to show deep love for each other, for love makes up for many of your faults."
　　　　　　　　　　　　　　　　　　　　1 Peter 4:8

I remember a lady who came to me for counseling a few years ago. She said, "Dr. Schuller, I'm getting a divorce."

Well, I didn't know him, and I didn't know her, so I proceeded to ask her some questions. "Does he drink too much?" She answered, "No, thank God he doesn't drink or I'd have left him long ago." "Well, does he gamble?" I asked. "Oh, no," she said, "he's never gambled. None of our friends gamble." I said, "Does he run around with other women?" She looked at me and said, "Do you think I'd be married to a guy like that? Of course not."

I continued, "Does he beat up the kids?" "No," she replied, "I have to say he's really nice with the children." I said, "Well, what's the matter then. He probably doesn't work regularly, is that it?" She said, "He's a good provider, and I have to give him credit for that." I pressed on, "Let's see. He doesn't drink, doesn't gamble, he works hard, doesn't beat you up, and you say he goes to church with you?" She said, "But only if I go will he go along." "Lady," I continued, "I've got news for you. If you let him go, I know twenty women who will grab him just like that." (She went out of there convinced she had a pretty good guy!)

There's no doubt about it, love looks for the best.

> I want the power of God to enter me
> so that I will become a true optimist!

Love Conquers Fear

"For I live in eager expectation and hope that I will never do anything that will cause me to be ashamed of myself; but that I will always be ready to speak out boldly for Christ. . . ."

Philippians 1:20

Robert Young, a Presbyterian pastor, told me this story. "One day a minister came in to see me and he was depressed. He said, 'I had a funeral yesterday for a beautiful Christian woman.' I couldn't understand why that had gotten him down and said so. He responded, 'Frankly, it was the way I treated the woman who died. I was affected by gossip. Someone told me, "She doesn't come to church anymore. She used to be such a faithful worker and so active, but she stopped coming to church about three years ago, and has she changed! She's always lounging around in expensive perfume, with a glass of liquor in reach. And once a week a strange man with an out-of-town license plate visits her."

"'When she suddenly died, her husband came to me to arrange the funeral service. I told him what I had heard. He was shocked! "My wife," he explained, "had an incurable fatal disease that hit her three years ago! She bought perfumes to cover the odor, the sheer negligees so the weight of the clothing would not hurt her abdomen, and the 'liquor' was bonafide medicine. The man who visited her was a specialist from out of town. She was a beautiful Christian to the end." ' "

> **Jesus, live in my life so
> I will believe the best first.**

Love Conquers Fear

"Love is always eager to believe the best."

1 Corinthians 13:7

There are two kinds of people in the world: those who build walls, and those who build bridges.

People who expect the worst from others create a mental climate of defensiveness and hostility. They become wall builders. But people who expect good to come out of others, who are eager to believe the best, are bridge builders.

If Jesus Christ really lives in your heart and life, you will be possessed by a love that will cause you to believe the best in the worst of times, in the worst of people, and in the worst of situations. *Love is eager to believe the best!*

As frustrating situations occur in your life, practice this principle. Look for the positive side. Accentuate the good aspects. And always remember, Jesus is there to help.

**Thank You, Lord, for giving me the strength
to believe the best in the worst conditions.**

Love Conquers Fear

"So don't be afraid; you are worth more than many sparrows."
Matthew 10:31

A person becomes a beautiful Christian, not because he's against something or afraid of some place, but because he's in love with someone. And I'm in love with Jesus Christ!

If you become a Christian because you're in love with Him, your faith has a positive taproot and that makes all the difference in your religion.

Fear produces horrible results. Anger produces disastrous results. But love produces miraculous rewards. Become a Christian not because of a threat but because of love.

In a pastor's office recently I saw a little prayer that said, "Lord, today help me to make my words tender and sweet. Because tomorrow I may have to eat them."

It is true—what you put out always comes back to you. Love produces miraculous rewards

> **I'm a Christian because
> I love Jesus Christ.**

Love Conquers Fear

"Each man should give what he has decided in his heart to give, not reluctantly or under compulsion, for God loves a cheerful giver."

2 Corinthians 9:7

Get rid of fear. Fall in love with a Person called Christ. You'll really come alive. And with His Spirit in your life, my favorite prayer will become your favorite prayer, too. It's the prayer of St. Francis of Assisi:

Lord, make me an instrument of Thy Peace;
Where there is hatred, let me sow love;
Where there is injury, pardon;
Where there is doubt, faith;
Where there is despair, hope;
Where there is darkness, light;
Where there is sadness, joy;
O Divine Master, grant that I may not so much seek to be consoled, as to console; to be understood, as to understand; to be loved, as to love;
For it is in giving, that we receive;
It is in pardoning, that we are pardoned;
It is in dying, that we are born to eternal life.

**Real love produces
real miracles!**

Love Expects the Best

"Fear of man is a dangerous trap, but to trust in God means safety."

Proverbs 29:25

To those of you who desire a better life, prepare to enter a new world! You do need one ingredient, however, and that's a spirit of adventure. A little nerve. We all have an inclination to seek the shelter of the familiar. And we have all kinds of built-in resistance against moving into an unknown aspect of life. Frequently we fear to adventure into new areas because adventures often mean getting familiar with the unfamiliar.

Are you afraid of religion? Maybe you don't talk "religious." Do you feel you don't know how to talk to God? The truth is, you don't have to speak the religious language to have a great religious adventure. Don't worry about religious lingo. You don't need to worry about phrases like, "Praise the Lord" and "I'm saved."

Are you afraid of Christianity because you've known people who seem hypocritical or narrow or negative? Maybe they were afraid of going to hell and were looking for an escape. Or maybe they accepted religion because they feared the world situations. The problem with many of those so-called Christians is that the taproot of their religion is negative instead of positive. *They have accepted a religion but haven't established a relationship.*

I will enter into the adventure of Christianity with a positive heart!

Love Expects the Best

"He is for me! How can I be afraid? What can mere man do to me?"

Psalms 118:6

Perfect love casts out all kinds of negative forces. Selfish love, however, produces fear. If I love you because I need you, or I love you because I want you, I'm going to be afraid that I might not get you; and then I'll have lost something I wanted to gain. But if you love because you want to give something to somebody, you'll never become fearful or worried or tense. For a giving love can never lose. *If they take what you offer, you'll succeed! If they don't take it, you've still got it! Either way, you can't lose!*

Selfish love builds walls. Robert Frost once said, "Before you build walls, make sure you know what you're walling out and what you're walling in."

Unselfish love builds bridges, which brings people closer together and unites the family of God.

**I feel myself becoming less selfish. Today
I will build bridges instead of walls.**

Love Expects the Best

"Dear friends, let us practice loving each other, for love comes from God and those who are loving and kind show that they are children of God, and that they are getting to know him better."

1 John 4:7

A member of our church who had heard me talk about the method of letting Christ's love flow through to a person you can't love told the following story.

"One morning I went to work remembering what you said. The first person I saw coming into my store was the salesman I could not stand! I saw him drive up to the curb; I knew his car. I saw him get out of that car. And I was already in a bad mood! My secretary, who also goes to this church and heard the same sermon said, 'Maybe you'd better try shooting him with prayers.' So before he got in I reached one hand in the air and with the other one I pointed at him through the window. He was gawking at me as if I were nuts.

"Later on he told me he thought I was going to change a light bulb. But I was saying, 'Jesus, I can't love that guy. I can't even stomach him. But You can. You love him, Jesus.' And the most amazing thing happened, I looked at the man's face and it had a countenance about it I had never noticed before. He looked congenial. *It worked. I ended up loving this guy!"*

I know You can work in my life this way too, Lord. Today I will try to let You love someone I just cannot love by myself.

> **Jesus, through me love those
> I cannot love.**

Love Expects the Best

"Yes, you must be a new and different person, holy and good. Clothe yourself with this new nature."

Ephesians 4:24

Discover this truth: Your belief and your expectations tend to set into motion the very forces that cause to come to pass what you are believing and what you are expecting. In other words, if you let a person know that you believe he or she is a beautiful person, they will become beautiful people! You give them a new self-image of what they are!

Two kinds of birds fly over the California deserts, the hummingbird and the vulture. All the vulture sees is rotten meat; that's what he's looking for. But the hummingbird doesn't see the carcass. Instead, it spots the blooming cactus flowers hidden behind the rocks. Each one finds what it looks for.

If you are eager to believe the best about people, they will become what you expect. You set in force psychological laws of dynamics. A psychology professor once said, *"Ultimately I am not what I think I am. I am not what you think I am. I am what I think you think I am."*

> **I will set the positive psychological laws in motion by thinking well of others!**

Love Expects the Best

"If then you have been raised with Christ, seek the things that are above, where Christ is."

Colossians 3:1

Jesus Christ went to the scum of the earth. He believed the best about them, and He let them know that He believed they were going to become the salt of the earth and the light of the world. He told them they were fishers of men and the leaders of a great international movement of love and brotherhood. And, wow! They ended up believing it, because He believed it!

When Jesus looks at you, He doesn't see what you are. *He sees what you can become.* And we must learn to see the potential within ourselves.

> **With You, Lord, I can do great things!
> I feel excited!**

Love Expects the Best

"Out of his glorious, unlimited resources he will give you the mighty inner strengthening of his Holy Spirit."

Ephesians 3:16

Frank Leahy, a famous coach of Notre Dame, faced his greatest challenge when his team played Southern Methodist at the Cotton Bowl, in Dallas, Texas, some years ago. At that time Notre Dame had not been beaten in four years, and the score was 20-20. There were one minute and twenty-eight seconds left to go in the game. He realized they were facing the biggest problem they had faced in four years. The crowd was ferocious. It was a miserable situation. Frank knew he had to relax his team, so he called for time. The quarterback came running over to him and said, "Do you have any words of wisdom you would like to give to the boys, Coach?" Frank looked at him and said, "Yes, tell them never to become a coach."

The team went into a huddle. The quarterback whispered something to them. All heads went back, there was a burst of laughter, and they ran onto the field. Southern Methodist kicked off and Notre Dame took the ball. One first down, another first down, and another, until they charged down the field and won the game. Leahy said, "You know, I've always believed that our worst time has within it the possibility of being our best time." Think of that!

**I will try to recognize the possibilities
in the worst of times.**

Love Expects the Best

"Be kind to each other, tenderhearted, forgiving one another, just as God has forgiven you because you belong to Christ."
Ephesians 4:32

Mom Schug is a lady in our church. She's kind of adopted me because I'm the same age as her only son who was killed when a Japanese kamikaze pilot crashed into his U.S. Navy carrier during World War II.

One day I read about a Japanese kamikaze pilot who was converted to Jesus Christ. His whole life was changed, and he was filled with love where once had been hate. So I invited him to give his testimony in our church, and Mom Schug was turned off. "That's one thing," she said sternly, "I will not hear."

I'll never forget the Sunday when that Japanese man was in the pulpit. I was very surprised to see Mom Schug sitting in a pew. She had come after all. Even though she listened, I could see she was tense.

The congregation was so impressed with him, they flocked to greet him after the service. When everyone had left, Mom Schug went up to this Japanese man. She whispered something to him, and his head went back as if he were shocked and hurt. Then I saw his head move forward. His arms went down and her arms went up. They hugged and cried. Christ lived in their hearts. Do you know any other religion that can help people to love like that?

**My heart is overflowing with
love and forgiveness!**

Love: the Source of Joy

*"For, after all, the important thing for us as Christians is not
what we eat or drink but stirring up goodness and peace and
joy from the Holy Spirit."*

Romans 14:17

What is the secret of real joy? Christians know the answer.
The real Christian knows the secret of real joy is the love
that tumbles up from deep within your heart and soul; when
you tear yourself loose from selfishness and bear the burdens of someone else, caring enough to share yourself with
him. Then love becomes *activated* and gives you the results
of *JOY!* So love is the secret of real joy.

Each of us distinguishes ourselves as individuals. Some
have special talents. Others are especially attractive. Still
others accomplish astounding achievements. But Christians
should all be distinguished by the love they give away. It
bursts forth with such enthusiasm. It can never be hidden.
You won't even have to tell people that you love Jesus
Christ. You won't be able to keep it secret, for love will give
you away!

**My prayer is that my love will make an obvious
statement about the kind of Christian I am!**

Love: the Source of Joy

"I have told you this so that you will be filled with joy. Yes your cup of joy will overflow."

John 15:11

I believe the fruit of joy is self-love. Freud said, "It is the will to pleasure that is important." Adler said, "No, it is the will to power." Frankl said, "It is the will to meaning." Fromm would say, "It is the will to love and to be loved." But I believe it is the will to self-love.

The will to pleasure is a frenetic attempt to escape from facing up to yourself.

The will to power is the foolish thought that with power you can manipulate people and thereby earn respect from them . . . a distorted attempt to build self-love.

The will to meaning loses meaning if it does not feed one's self-respect.

The will to love and be loved is the "good feeling." It is the beginning of self-love.

Self-love is realizing that God is a part of us. And our limited humanness, with all its pitfalls, misjudgments, and temptations is fantastic when God is in it.

**Thank You, Lord, for lifting me to Your level.
With Your help, I can be great!**

Love: the Source of Joy

"Thou wilt show me that path of life: in thy presence is fullness of joy; at thy right hand there are pleasures for evermore."
Psalms 16:11

How can you get the kind of love inside you that will help you to have real joy? Let's talk about it in terms of a five-pointed Star of Joy. In the heart of the star is a cross, which represents Jesus Christ. When He is in your heart, it becomes the heart of the Star of Joy.

The first point of the star is Conceive. Conceive of the fact that maybe it is possible for Christ to come into your life. Take the A out of Christian, and you have Christ—in.

Christ in me. Conceive that it is possible for you to actually become a human being in whom Jesus Christ's Spirit can enter.

Once during a party game where everyone was choosing whom they would like to be reincarnated as, Dick Van Dyke said, "It may sound corny, but I'd like to be reincarnated as Jesus." There was a great pause.

Everyone would like to come back as Jesus. The good news I have for you is *it's possible!* Conceive of it! What the mind of man can see, the mind of God can achieve. It begins with that consciousness, that higher consciousness, that Christ can come and live in you!

I know You are a part of me, God. You live
in spirit. Thank You.

Love: the Source of Joy

"But as many as received him to them gave he power to become sons of God."

John 1:12

The second point of the star is Receive. The Bible makes it very clear that if you ask Jesus Christ to come into your life, He will do it. That's a fact. The Bible teaches it. And I know it works!

Receiving Christ into your life is an act of the intellect. It is an act of the will, not an act of the heart. It is not emotional; it is volitional.

The third point of the star is Believe. After you have conceived and received Christ into your life, don't expect clouds to explode. Don't look for a feeling. *Just Believe!*

God does not promise your eyes will fill up with tears and your heart will burst with emotion. He promises to act on faith, not on feeling.

> **I will try to respond to Your word, Lord,
> not to my feelings.**

Love: the Source of Joy

"They that sow in tears, reap in joy!"

Psalms 126:5

The fourth point of the star is Relieve. Relieve your mind of all negative thoughts—fear, hate, doubt, suspicion, hostility, unbelief. Doubt and faith do not harmonize. Nor do righteousness and sin. If there is any secret lust, sin, hate, hostility, prejudice, or fear in your mind, get rid of it.

One dead spider in the thermostat at the base of the stairs in our sanctuary knocked out our whole air conditioning system one summer. If a dead spider can do that, what do you think one prejudice, hate, or lust thought that you hang on to can do to your five-pointed star?

The fifth point of the star is Actchieve. The word achieve is misspelled deliberately. ACT-chieve. Be like a sprinkler head and let the water sprinkle through. Be like a fountain pen and let Christ, like beautiful ink, write His message through your life.

> I allow God to drain away all negative thoughts.
> My relations are an expression of
> God's healing powers!

Love: the Source of Joy

"There I will go to the altar of God, my exceeding joy, and praise him with my harp."

Psalms 43:4

1. Conceive
2. Receive
3. Believe
4. Relieve
5. Actchieve

Affirm with me now the following five points of our Star of Joy:

1. I *conceive* that Christ can actually live within me.
2. I *receive* Him into my life now.
3. I *believe* that He is there even if I don't feel it.
4. I *relieve* myself of my secret sins.
5. I will *act* and *achieve* joyful Christian living this week.

Remember: *Love is a magic candle—it grows longer the longer you burn it.*

> **The joy of the Lord
> is my strength!**

Love: the Source of Joy

*"Then make me truly happy by loving each other, working to-
gether with one heart and mind and purpose."*

Philippians 2:2

Whenever I visit a sick friend, or help someone who is
hurting, a beautiful emotion from the depth of my soul
overtakes me. It is positive. It is nurturing. I call it joy. The
only way you can get it is when you really lose yourself,
honestly caring about someone who needs help.

I believe the secret and source of real joy is real love,
which tears you from your own projects to care about someone else. Bearing another's burdens. Sharing yourself with
another person alone. In prayerful moments. In tearful moments. In happy moments. Truly being an instrument of
God's love. When you have reached this place in your
Christian walk, you will understand what Matthew meant in
chapter 2, verse 10;

"Their joy knew no bounds!"

**My faith is strong because I am filled with
the joy of the Lord!**

Love: the Greatest Gift

"Behold, I stand at the door and knock; if any one hears my voice and opens the door, I will come in to him and eat with him, and he with me."

Revelation 3:20

What really happened on Christmas? Love came and knocked at the door of the earth's heart. And how did people react to it? They reacted just as they still respond to love today, in one of the following four ways:

1. *Many ignored it.* When love knocked at their door, many ignored it. They were people who were too busy. How often have you missed your doorbell because the vacuum cleaner was going, the television set was too loud, or the children were making too much noise. Later someone told you, "I rang your doorbell, but nobody answered."

In A.D. 78 a very old man was sitting in his hut outside a town called Bethlehem. A teenage boy came running to him and said, "Ismael, Ismael, I just heard that you were one of the shepherds on the hill many years ago when Jesus was born. Tell me what did the baby look like? Did you see His parents? Was it really so crowded?" The old man played with the furrows of his brow, then he ran his fingers through his straggly, white beard. His eyes misted, then became wet. His lips trembled and he answered, "Yes, I was with those shepherds. But I was so busy taking care of the sheep, I didn't bother to go and look. I never saw Him."

When the Lord knocks on the do⟋
I will not be too busy⟋

Love: the Greatest Gift

"I will give you one heart and a new spirit; I will take from you your hearts of stone and give you tender hearts of love for God."

Ezekiel 11:19

2. *Some deplored it.* When love knocked at their door, some deplored it. They hardened their hearts. Because they had been hurt once, they couldn't bring themselves to dare to try and take another chance. So they deplore love. They became negative in their attitude toward love.

Insecure people are afraid to love. Angry people do not dare to love; they might lose their hostilities. Selfish people can't risk love; it may cause them to begin sharing!

The innkeeper in Bethlehem the night of Christ's birth said, "Oh, no, not somebody else. I'm full enough as it is. I don't have room for any more people." All he saw was another problem when he saw a pregnant woman, a man, and a donkey. He *deplored* it. His place was overcrowded already. What he didn't realize was that in God's providence, problems always come as real opportunities. Only we may not recognize them. God was planning a beautiful surprise for the world, and the innkeeper didn't know it.

soft and tender, Lord, so that I
to love like You.

Love: the Greatest Gift

"But if we are living in the light of God's presence, just as Christ does, then we have wonderful fellowship and joy with each other, and the blood of Jesus his son cleanses us from every sin."

1 John 1:7

When love comes knocking at your door, don't ignore or deplore it, but . . .

3. Explore it! Give it a chance.

Think of the shepherds. They said, "Let us go even unto Bethlehem and see this wonderful thing that has happened." And there were the three wisemen who said, "Let us go to a far off land and see if this is true."

Are you willing to explore the Christian faith? Really explore it? Don't let your hurts keep you from exploring Him. Don't let your set mind keep you from hearing the truth. Don't be a stubborn doubter. Are you willing to be a believer if that's what God wants? Explore it!

And you will find, like anyone who comes close to Christ finds, He is wonderful!

> **Jesus, help me to explore all the wonderful facets of You!**

Love: the Greatest Gift

"Mary asked the angel, 'But how can I have a baby? I am a virgin.' The angel replied, 'The Holy Spirit shall come upon you, and the power of God shall overshadow you; so the baby born to you will be utterly holy—the Son of God."

Luke 1:34,35

After you have explored love, you will *adore Jesus Christ*. As the angels and the shepherds and millions through the years have ... believe me! Since today commemorates His birth, let us sing and adore our Lord.

> Oh, come all ye faithful, joyful and triumphant.
> Oh, come ye; Oh, come ye to Bethlehem.
> Come and behold Him; Born the King of angels.
> Oh, come, let us adore Him.
> Oh, come, let us adore Him.
> Oh, come, let us adore Him, Christ the Lord.

Happy Birthday, Jesus.
Thank You God for Your wonderful Gift!

Love: the Greatest Gift

"I am come a light into the world, that whosoever believeth on me should not abide in darkness."

John 12:46

Do you know what impresses me the most about Christmas? The fantastic potential in the most unlikely child. Consider the tremendous possibilities in a person whose life has been touched by God.

When Jesus was born, there was no living person on planet earth who would have guessed that two thousand years later there would be 900 million people in the world who would claim to be followers of that baby, born in that ignominious place. Yet today, with jet airplanes flying around the world, an American flag flying on the moon, and the penetration of outer space by satellites that continue sending messages to planet earth long after they've been launched, Jesus Christ is more widely known and greater than ever before.

**I am an instrument of
God's potential and possibilities.**

Love: the Greatest Gift

"We are no longer Jews or Greeks or slaves or free men or even merely men or women, but we are all the same—we are Christians; we are one in Christ Jesus."

Galatians 3:28

Who was Jesus Christ? A human being? Or a Divine Incarnation of the Son of God, as Christians have taught through the centuries? Have the Christians all been hoodwinked, duped, psyched out and fooled? Or have they seen right? I submit this is the most important question you can raise today.

I happen to believe the Christians were right. I believe this because of my respect for the Jewish tradition. They prophesied there would be a time when God would come, in human form, into human history. Centuries before the birth of Jesus it was prophesied that when the Messiah was born, He would come from the tribe of David. Second, that He would be born in Bethlehem. Third, that He would be despised and rejected by men and be crucified. Finally, that He would rise from the dead and head a spiritual kingdom.

Hundreds of years after these prophecies were made, Jesus was born in Bethlehem. Do you see the miracle of it all? Miracle of miracles, traveling day after day, on a slow donkey, Mary did not deliver until they got to Bethlehem. When she arrived, her baby was born.

> **The splendor of Your miracles, Lord, takes my breath away.**

Love: the Greatest Gift

"In all thy ways acknowledge Him, and He shall direct thy paths."

Proverbs 3:6

Another reason I believe that Christ is the Messiah is because of His own character. He has never been surpassed as an example of an emotionally healthy human. Spiritually, he was positive, never negative. He was honest, open, and totally reliable. Show me a human being who is emotionally mature, mentally healthy, spiritually positive, honest, open, and reliable, and I say there's a person you can believe when he speaks.

So what did He say about Himself? He said:

"I am the way, the truth, and the life; no man cometh unto the Father, but by me" (John 14:6).

"I am the door: by me if any man enter in, he shall be saved" (John 10:9).

When He went before the council and they asked Him, "Are you then the Son of God?" He replied, "You are right in saying I am" (Luke 22:70).

I will try to follow Your perfect example, Jesus, Son of God!

Love: the Greatest Gift

"You search the Scriptures, for you believe they will give you eternal life. And the Scriptures point to me! Yet you won't come to me so that I can give you this life eternal!"

John 5:39,40

Why was Jesus born? To reveal the reality of God to the human race and to tell us that life is eternal.

If you were an invisible god who couldn't be put under a test tube, immaterial, not made out of flesh, bones, meat, and blood, how would you reveal yourself to creatures that had bones, meat, hair, blood, and brains? You would have to reveal yourself through a revelation.

Let's suppose you were a god and you wanted to reveal yourself to a flock of birds. How would you do it? You'd probably become a bird. If you were a god and you wanted to reveal yourself to human beings, what would you do? You'd become a human being. And that is what happened.

Jesus Christ's birth was a once-in-history-act when the God who created the world fulfilled His moral obligation to all of us and revealed the spiritual truth we would never know through empirical knowledge. Truth we could only come to understand through a revelation. So God revealed Himself in the person of Jesus Christ.

> **Thank you, God, for revealing Yourself in a way that we could all understand.**

Love: the Greatest Gift

"He that heareth my word, and believeth on Him that sent me, hath everlasting life, and shall not come into condemnation; but is passed from death unto life."

John 5:24

What are you doing about the fact of Jesus Christ? Of all the books you will ever read in your life, of all the lectures you will ever hear, of all the professors, philosophers, teachers, preachers, priests, rabbis, and ministers you will ever listen to, nobody ever again will ask you a more important question than "What are you going to do about this fact of Christ?"

Truly the gates of heaven and hell were in His hands and the destiny of your immortal soul is in His hands.

Thank God He has allowed spiritual truth to come to us through faith. I invite you by an act of faith to receive His gift of spiritual wisdom and understanding.

> **Reach out to me, Lord,
> with Your gift of spiritual wisdom.**

Love: the Greatest Gift

*"There are three things that remain—faith, hope, and love—
and the greatest of these is love."*

1 Corinthians 13:13

A cynic would say, "If there is one thing that is sure and
certain, it is that nothing is sure and certain."

But there is something that does not change! And that
something is man. Every human being born needs to eat,
breathe, and drink water, or he will die. The body does not
change in its demands. Nor does the heart of man change.
Every heart needs the food of human love.

What is that deep yearning in your heart? Are there times
when your heart almost seems moist in its crying out for
nourishment? What is it that you need deep in your soul?
We use the words heart hunger to describe the feeling. Your
heart needs love and God is able to give it to you—all you
will ever need.

Remember:

No problem is too big for God's power;
No person is too small for God's love.

**I receive God's total love.
I feel complete and whole.**